The Seagull Sartre Library

The Seagull Sartre Library

The Seagull Sartre Library

VOLUME 6
VENICE AND ROME

JEAN-PAUL SARTRE

TRANSLATED BY
CHRIS TURNER

LONDON NEW YORK CALCUTTA

INDIA

This work is published with the support of
Institut français en Inde – Embassy of France in India

✳

Seagull Books, 2021

Originally published in Jean-Paul Sartre,
Situations IV © Éditions Gallimard, Paris, 1964

These essays were first published in English translation
by Seagull Books in *Portraits* (2009)
English translation © Christ Turner, 2009

ISBN 978 0 8574 2 909 4

British Library Cataloguing-in-Publication Data
A catalogue record for this book is available
from the British Library

Typeset by Seagull Books, Calcutta, India
Printed and bound in the USA by Integrated Books International

CONTENTS

THE CAPTIVE OF VENICE

The Wiles of Jacopo

Nothing. The life has sunk without trace. A few dates, a few facts and then the prattling of old authors. But we should not be discouraged: *Venice speaks to us*; this false witness' voice, shrill at times, whispering at others, broken by silences, is its voice. In the story of Tintoretto, a portrait of the artist painted in his lifetime by his native city, an unrelenting animosity shows through. The City of the Doges tells us she has taken a serious dislike to the most famous of her sons. Nothing is said openly: there are hints and suggestions and then it is on to other matters. Yet this unyielding hatred is as insubstantial as sand; it is not so much an open aversion as a coldness, a sullenness, the insidious dispersal of a rejection. And we ask no more: Jacopo fought a dubious fight against his countless enemies, was wearied by it and died defeated. That, in broad outline, was his life. We shall see the whole of it, in its sombre nakedness, if we sweep aside for a moment the undergrowth of tittle-tattle that blocks our access.

Jacopo was born in 1518. His father was a dyer. Venice immediately whispers in our ear that this was a very bad beginning: 'Around 1530, the boy entered Titian's studio as an apprentice, but, a few days later, the famous quinquagenarian saw genius in him and showed him the door.' Short and snappy, as accounts go. This anecdote recurs repeatedly, with an insistence that eventually seems conclusive. Titian doesn't come out of it well, you may say. And he doesn't, at least not *today*, not as *we* see things. But when Vasari narrated this anecdote in 1567, Titian had reigned for half a century: nothing is more respectable than a long period of impunity. And then, by the rules of the day, he was second in authority only to God in his own studio: no one would deny him the right to throw out a hireling. On the contrary, it is the victims who are presumed guilty: branded by misfortune, they have the evil eye—perhaps infectiously. In short, this is the first time an unhappy childhood figures in the *légende dorée* of Italian painting. I feel sure there is something to be made of this, but we shall come back to it later. The Voice of Venice never lies, provided one knows how to hear it; we shall listen to it when we have learnt better how to do so. For the time being, whatever may be the deeper truth, we must stress the implausibility of the facts.

Titian wasn't an easy man to get on with. That much is known. But Jacopo was twelve years old. At twelve, a 'gift' is nothing; the slightest thing can destroy it. Patience and time are needed to consolidate a fragile facility and turn it into talent. And even the touchiest of artists is not, at the height of his fame, going to take offence at a mere boy. But let us suppose the Master did jealously dismiss his apprentice. This is tantamount to killing him: to be cursed by a 'national treasure' is a very serious matter. All the more so as Titian did not have the frankness to make his true motives known: he was king, he frowned and all doors were closed to the black sheep thereafter; the very profession of painter was denied him.

It is not every day you see a child on a blacklist. Our interest is aroused and we'd like to know how he overcame such a dreadful eventuality. But all in vain: in every one of the books, the thread of the narrative breaks off at this point; we run up against a wall of silence—no one will tell us what became of him between the ages of twelve and twenty. Some have tried to fill the gap by imagining he taught himself to paint. But this at least we know to have been impossible, and past writers knew it better than we do: in the early sixteenth century, the art of painting was still a complex craft, hedged about by ceremony, beset by a welter of recipes and rituals: it was more a skill than a branch of knowledge, a set of procedures rather than a method, while everything—professional rules, traditions and trade secrets—combined to make apprenticeship a social obligation and a necessity. The biographers' silence betrays their embarrassment; incapable of reconciling the precocious fame of young Robusti[1] with his excommunication, they cast a veil over the eight years that separate the two. We may take this as an admission: no one threw Jacopo out. Since he did not die of boredom and pique in his father's dye-shop, he must have worked properly, normally, in the studio of a painter of whom we know nothing, except that that painter *was not* Titian. In distrustful, tight-knit societies, hatred is retroactive; if the mysterious beginnings of this life seem a premonition of its mysterious end, if the curtain that went up on a miraculously interrupted disaster comes down on an unmiraculous one, this is because Venice has arranged everything retrospectively to mark out the child for the old age that was to be his. Nothing happens and nothing lasts; birth is the mirror of death; between the two lies scorched earth; everything is eaten away by bad luck.

Let us move beyond these mirages; on the farther side, the view is clear and reaches to the horizon: what emerges is an adolescent who starts off in top gear and races towards glory. As early as 1539, Jacopo has left his master and set up on his own: he has *his own studio*. The young employer has gained his independence, fame and

---

1 Until quite recently, it was thought that Tintoretto's real name was Jacopo Robusti and this assumption informs the whole of Sartre's text. It is now believed that Robusti was a nickname and that the family name was actually Comin. [Trans.]

clients; he is taking on workers and apprentices in his turn. Make no mistake: in a city teeming with painters, where an economic crisis is threatening to stifle the market, to become a master at twenty is the exception. Merit alone cannot bring this, nor hard work and worldly wisdom; it takes a degree of good fortune. And everything is running in Robusti's favour: Paolo Caliari is ten years old, Titian is sixty-two.[2] Between the unknown child and an old man who will surely not be around for much longer, a lot of good painters are to be found, but only Tintoretto seems bound for excellence: in his own generation, at least, he has no equal, so the road ahead is clear. And, indeed, for a few years he makes untroubled headway: commissions flow in, he is popular with public, patricians and connoisseurs; Aretino deigns to compliment him personally; the young man has the preternatural gifts that Providence reserves for those adolescents who will die young.

But he does not die and his troubles begin. Titian turns out to be appallingly long-lived and displays elaborate malicious intent towards his young challenger. The old monarch is so spiteful as to designate his successor officially and, as one might have expected, that successor was Veronese. Aretino's condescension turns to bitterness; the critics nip, bite, scratch and howl; in a word, they become modernized. This would not matter at all if Jacopo still had the public's esteem. But suddenly the

---

2 Paolo Caliari is better known as Veronese. [Trans.]

wheel turns. At thirty years of age, confident in his own powers, he comes into his own: he paints *St Mark Saving the Slave*, putting the whole of himself into the work. To astonish, to hit hard and take the world by storm—this was very much his style. For once, however, he will be the one to be disconcerted: the work stuns his contemporaries, but it scandalizes them. He finds he has zealous detractors, but not zealous defenders; one senses the presence of a cabal in the background: he is halted in his tracks.[3] As they square up to each other, both united and separated by a single malaise, Venice and its painter look each other in the eye and the understanding between them is gone. 'Jacopo,' says the city, 'has not fulfilled the promise of his adolescence.' And the artist says, 'The moment I revealed myself, they were disappointed. It wasn't *me* that they loved!' This misunderstanding degenerates into rancour on both sides: something is torn in the fabric of Venice.

1548 is the hinge year. *Before that date*, the gods were with him; *after it*, they were against him. No great misfortunes, just bad luck: you need to have a bellyful of it; the gods had smiled on the child the better to destroy the man. As a result, Jacopo changes into himself, becomes that frenzied, hunted outlaw, Tintoretto. Before this, we know nothing about him, except that he worked at breakneck speed: you cannot make a name

---

3 Ridolfi even claims that the Scuola San Marco rejected the canvas and Tintoretto had to take it back home.

for yourself at twenty without application. Afterwards, the application turns to rage; he wants to produce, to produce endlessly, to sell, to crush his rivals by the number and size of his paintings. There is something frantic in this upping of the pace: right up to his death, Robusti seems to be racing against the clock and it is impossible to say whether he is trying to find himself through work or flee himself in overwork. 'Greased-Lightning Tintoretto' sails under a pirate flag; for this speedy freebooter, all means are fair—with a marked preference for foul ones. Disinterested whenever disinterest pays, he lowers his eyes and refuses to quote a price, repeating like a lackey: 'You may pay whatever you like.' But lackeys are better placed than anyone to know that there's a tariff for carrying bags: they count on the client to fleece himself, out of generosity.

On other occasions, to secure a deal, he offers the merchandise at cost price: this bargain-basement contract will bring him other, more profitable ones. He learns that the Order of the *Crociferi* are to commission work from Paolo Caliari and, feigning ignorance of the fact, goes and offers them his services. They try to show him the door politely: 'We would be only too happy, but we want a Veronese.' 'A Veronese's an excellent idea,' he says, 'And who's going to paint you one?' 'But,' they reply with some surprise, 'We thought Paolo Caliari was just the man for the job . . .' To which Tintoretto, in turn astonished, replies: 'Caliari? What a strange idea. *I'*ll do you a better Veronese than him. And cheaper.' The deal is struck and he is as good as his word. Twenty times he repeats the trick: twenty times he 'does' *Pordenones* and *Titians*—and always at a knock-down price.

The question that tormented him was how he could lower the costs. One day he found the answer—a mean-minded solution of genius—and it was to overturn a whole tradition. It was customary for the masters to have their paintings copied; the studio executed replicas and sold them at highly competitive prices, which meant there was also a secondary market for painting. To capture this clientele, Jacopo proposed to offer it something both *better* and *cheaper*. He did so by eliminating the originals. His painters would take their inspiration from his canvases, but would not *imitate* them. By simple, unvarying methods, his co-workers would produce something new without invention. To do this, they had merely to reverse the composition, to put the left on the right and the right on the left, to replace a female figure with an old man taken from another picture, leaving the woman to be re-used elsewhere. These operations required some training, but they took no more time than mere copying. And Tintoretto was able guilelessly to proclaim: 'You can acquire an original from me for the price of a copy.'

When they didn't want his paintings, he made a present of them. On 31 May 1564, at the Scuola San Rocco, the Brotherhood's ruling body decided to brighten up its meeting hall: the central oval of the ceiling was to be decorated with a painting on canvas. Paolo Caliari, Jacopo Robusti, Schiavone, Salviati and Zuccaro were invited to submit sketches. Tintoretto bribed some servants and obtained the exact dimensions. He had already worked for the Brotherhood and I do not rule out the possibility that he even had accomplices within its governing *Banca e Zonta*. On the appointed day, each artist showed his drawing. When Robusti's turn came, the assembled company were thunderstruck: he climbed a ladder, removed a board and above their heads unveiled a stunning picture already finished and in place. Amid the rumblings of discontent, he explained: 'A sketch can be misleading. While I was at it, I preferred to complete the job. But if you don't like my work, Gentlemen, I shall make a present of it to you. Not to you, but to Saint Roch, your patron, who has shown me such kindness.' He had forced their hands and the old rogue knew it: the statutes of the Brotherhood forbade them to refuse any pious donation. All that remained was to register the event in the annals of the Scuola: 'On this day, the undersigned Jacopo Tintoretto, painter, has presented us with a picture: he asks no remuneration, undertakes to complete the work if required and declares himself satisfied.' And the 'undersigned', in his turn, writes: '*Io Jachomo Tentoretto pitor contento et prometo ut supra.*'

Contento? I'm sure he was! The donation spread panic among his competitors. It opened all the doors of the Scuola to him, delivering its immense, desert-like walls over to the furies of his brushwork and eventually bringing him an annual pension of a hundred ducats. So content was he, indeed, that he repeated the trick in 1571. At the Doges' Palace this time. The Signoria was looking to commemorate the Battle of Lepanto and had artists submit their competing sketches. Tintoretto brought a canvas and donated it. It was accepted with gratitude. Shortly afterwards, he sent them his bill.

The inclination will perhaps be to regard his shameful, though charming, craftiness as a feature of the age rather than of his character: Tintoretto wasn't personally a shark, but his century was one of sharp practice. In a way, this would not be wrong. If someone wished to condemn him on the strength of these anecdotes, I can see the defence that could be mounted. Beginning with the most serious argument: namely, that no one could at the time *work on his own account*. Today, painting is a picture sale; in those days, it was a painter market. They stood in the public square, like the *braccianti*[4] in the little towns of southern Italy; the buyers arrived, examined them all, choosing just one to take off to their church, *scuola* or *palazzo*. You had to offer yourself, put yourself about, the way our theatre directors do; you had to accept any old work, the way they accept any old script in the wild hope of using it to show off what they can do. Everything was fixed by contract: the subject, the

---

4 Day-labourers.

number, status and sometimes even poses of the figures depicted, the dimensions of the canvas; religious traditions and traditions of taste added their constraints. The clients had the moods and whims of our theatre producers; they also, sadly, had their sudden moments of inspiration: at a sign from them, the whole painting had to be redone. In the Medici palaces, Benozzo Gozzoli underwent long, exquisite torture at the hands of idiotic patrons;[5] where Tintoretto is concerned, one need only compare the *Paradise* in the Louvre with that in the Doges' Palace to see the degree of pressure he was under. Intransigence, a refusal to compromise and a proud self-imposed poverty didn't exist as possible solutions: the family had to be fed and the studio had to be kept running, the way machines have to be kept running today. In a word, you either had to paint to order or give up painting.

No one can blame Tintoretto for wanting to make money; certainly, in the middle years of his life he was rarely without work and there was no shortage of cash. This utilitarian's principle was that you don't do anything for nothing: painting would merely be a pastime if it didn't bring a monetary return. We shall see that, in later life, he bought himself a comfortable, plebeian residence in an unfashionable part of town. With this he had security; it was the crowning glory of his career. But

---

5 Benozzo Gozzoli (1421–97): a Florentine painter. In his early years, he was an assistant to Fra Angelico. [Trans.]

it took all his savings and the Robusti children were forced to share a paltry inheritance: the studio equipment, a waning clientele and the house itself, which went to the eldest son and then to the son-in-law. Twelve years after her husband's death, Faustina bitterly recalled that he had left his family in dire straits. She was right to complain: Tintoretto had always been a law unto himself about such things. There can be no doubt that he liked money, but he did so in the American way: he saw it merely as the outward mark of his success. Ultimately, this contract-chaser wanted just one thing: the means to carry on his profession. And then there was some justification for his dishonesties: they wouldn't even have been conceivable had he not at least had the upper hand in terms of professional skill, capacity for work, and speed. His 'sprinting' gave him his advantage: it took him as long to paint a good picture as others took to make bad sketches.

And if he plagiarized Veronese, Veronese did the same to him. We have to view their mutual borrowings as their contemporaries would have. For many of them, the great painters were mere trade names or corporate, legal persons. *We* want *this particular painting* first and foremost. And, through it, we get the whole man: we hang Matisse on our walls. But consider the *Crociferi*: they didn't care one whit for Caliari; they were after a certain style that suited their taste: a blissful stupidity, a pleasing splendour, and all trouble-free. They knew a trademark and a slogan: a picture signed by Veronese is a picture to set your mind at rest. That was what they wanted, nothing more. For his part, Caliari could do better and proved that he could: he painted an awe-inspiring Crucifixion.[6] But he was too good a business-man to overtax his genius. Given this state of affairs, it would be petty of us to blame Tintoretto for at times appropriating a style that belonged rightfully to no one. After all, he made an honest offer: 'You want mindless vivacity? I'll give it to you.'

I will happily concede all this. The point is not to judge him, but to establish whether his age felt itself unreservedly reflected in him. Now, the evidence on this score is quite plain: his methods shocked his contempo-raries and they held them against him. They may per-haps have put up with a degree of unfair competition, but Tintoretto went too far. All over Venice, the same cry could be heard: 'That's too much!' Even in this mer-chant city, this excessively shrewd merchant was regarded as eccentric. At the Scuola San Rocco, when he had blustered his way to the commission, his fellow painters cried 'foul' so loudly that he felt the need to pacify them. The building, he pointed out, had other ceilings and walls; the work was only just beginning; once his dona-tion was accepted he would slip away and leave the field to worthier men. Those unfortunate fellows didn't take

---

6 It hangs in the Louvre. The funniest part is that it was inspired by the real Robusti.

long to discover he had been lying in his teeth: the Scuola was to become his fiefdom and no other painter set foot in it in his lifetime.

And yet this surely wasn't the beginning of their hatred of him. We may note, however, that the scandal occurred in 1561 and the first *Life* of Tintoretto appeared in 1567: the proximity of the dates adds the final touch of explanation to the origins and meaning of the spiteful gossip collected by Vasari. Were these the slanders of jealous rivals? But all the painters were frantically jealous of each other; why would these slanders all be against Robusti if he were not the 'black sheep' of the artists, if he did not represent in everyone's eyes the faults of their neighbours all gathered together in one single person and carried to extremes? The clients themselves seemed shocked by his methods. Not all of them, admittedly. But he had made a great many firm enemies. Master Zammaria de Zignioni, a member of the Brotherhood of San Rocco, promised fifteen ducats towards the decoration costs on the express condition that Jacopo did not undertake the work. And the annals of the Brotherhood indicate that after Tintoretto's *coup*, the *Banca e Zonta* held some sensitive and rather stormy sessions in the Scuola itself, with the embarrassing donation gleaming above their heads. Agreement was reached, but Master de Zignioni kept his ducats. Nor did the public authorities always seem well-disposed towards him. Tintoretto donated his *Battle of Lepanto* in 1571; in 1577, the painting was destroyed by fire. When it came to replacing it, it seemed reasonable for its painter to assume the Signoria would call on him to do the job. But, not at all: he was deliberately passed over in favour of the second-rate Vicentino. It may perhaps have been argued that the picture had not been greatly liked. But this is barely plausible: Jacopo kept his nose clean when he worked for the authorities; he 'did a Titian' and kept himself out of it. Moreover, since 1571, the government had commissioned several works from him. No, it wasn't that the Venetian administration intended to forego his services altogether, but it wanted to punish him for his sharp practice. In short, all were in agreement: he was an unfair competitor, a rogue painter; there must have been something rotten about him to have no friends at all.

You troubled fine souls who make the dead serve the edification of the living—and your own edification in particular—may treat his excess, if you will, as striking proof of his passion. But the fact remains that passions are as varied as the people who have them: there are the consuming and the reflective, the dreamy and the concerned, the practical, the abstract, the idling, the precipitate and a hundred others. I would term Tintoretto's passion practical, concerned/recriminatory and consuming/precipitate. The more I think about his lamentable tricks, the more convinced I am that they originated in a sickened heart. What a nest of vipers! There is everything in that heart: the delirium of pride and the madness of humility, thwarted ambitions and limitless confusion, dynamism and bad luck, the will to 'make it' and the dizzying sense of failure. His life is the story of a social climber gnawed at by fear; it begins merrily, briskly, with a solidly mounted offensive and then, after the grave reverse of 1548, the pace speeds up to an insane, infernal degree; Jacopo will fight on until his death, but he knows he will not win. Social climbing and anxiety—these are the two biggest vipers in the nest. If we really want to know him, we must draw closer and take a look at them.

The Puritans of the Rialto

No one is cynical. To heap reproaches on oneself without becoming wholly downcast is the pastime of saints. But only up to a certain point: these chaste individuals condemn their lewdness, these generous people denounce their avarice, but if they discover what is really blighting them—namely, saintliness—then, like all guilty men, they run for justifications. Tintoretto is not a saint; he knows the whole city frowns on his methods; if he stubbornly persists in them, this is because he feels *he* is in the right. But do not tell me he is conscious of his genius: genius, that foolish wager, knows what it dares but doesn't know its own worth. Nothing could be more wretched than that fretful temerity that longs for the moon and dies without ever having reached it: pride comes first, unproven, unauthorized; when it becomes frenzied, you may call it genius if you will, but I don't really see what is to be gained by that. No: Tintoretto doesn't justify his roguishness either by the limited fullness of his skill or by the infinite void of his aspirations:

he is defending his rights. Each time a commission goes to one of his colleagues, he feels a wrong is being done to him. He must be given his head: he will cover all the city's walls with his paintings. No *campo* will be too vast, no *sotto portico* too obscure for him not to wish to adorn them; he will plaster the ceilings with his pictures, passers-by will walk upon his finest images, his brush will spare neither the facades of the palazzi on the Grand Canal nor the gondolas, nor perhaps even the gondoliers. He is a man who feels he has received, as a birthright, the privilege of transforming his city into himself and we may argue, in a sense, that he is right.

When he begins his apprenticeship, painting is in a bad way. Florence is in open crisis. Venice, as is its wont, is saying nothing or lying. But we have clear proof that the sources of properly Rialtine inspiration have dried up. In the late fifteenth century, the city was deeply affected by Antonello da Messina's stays there: this is the decisive turning-point; from that point on, it imports its painters. I don't say it goes very far to look for them: but the most renowned of them come, nonetheless, from *terra firma*: Giorgione from Castelfranco, Titian from Pieve di Cadore, Paolo Caliari and Bonifazio dei Pitati from Verona, Palma Vecchio from Bergamo, Girolamo the Elder and Paris Bordone from Treviso, and Andrea Schiavone from Zara. And there are others I could mention. In actual fact, this aristocratic republic is, first and foremost, a technocracy; it always had the audacity to recruit its specialists from anywhere and the shrewdness to treat them as its own children. Moreover, this is the period when *la Serenissima*, thwarted on the seas and threatened by coalitions on the mainland, turns its attention to its hinterland and attempts to shore up its power by conquest: the new immigrants are, for the most part, natives of the annexed territories. All the same, with this massive importation of talent, Venice was betraying its unease. When you remember that most of the artists of the Quattrocento were born within its walls or at Murano, you cannot help thinking that the line could not have been carried on, after the Vivarini and Bellini families died out and after the death of Carpaccio, without an infusion of new blood.

Painting is like other trades: it was the patricians who made it easy for good craftsmen to come in; it was the patricians, demonstrating what we might call a cosmopolitan chauvinism, who saw the Republic of the Doges as a kind of melting pot. In the view of that jealous, distrustful aristocracy, foreigners made the best Venetians: if they adopted Venice, they did so because they had fallen in love with it; if they wanted to be adopted by it, they would tend to be compliant. But the local craftsmen certainly didn't see the newcomers the same way. And why should they? It was foreign competition. They were not so unwise as to protest and were outwardly welcoming, but there were still conflicts and, indeed, perpetual tensions and a resentful pride. Forced to bow to the foreigners' technical superiority, the native disguised his humiliation by insisting the more strongly on his prerogatives; he agreed to give way to the more expert, more skilful craftsman, but he did so as a sacrifice for the homeland: his rights remained intact. A Rialtan was *on home ground* in Venice; German workers were better at glassblowing, but they would never have the Venetian's birthright. Before they passed on, the great painters of the Quattrocento had the bitter experience of seeing public taste desert them in favour of young incomers who held them in contempt. That foreigner Titian, for example, when he left one of the Bellini brothers for the other (Gentile for Giovanni), did so because he was in pursuit of another foreigner, Antonello, that meteor who had rent the sky of Venice and parted the waters of its lagoon twenty years before. In Giovanni himself Tiziano Vecelli was not interested at all: what he sought in him was a reflection. We have proof of this in the fact that he very quickly left the master for his disciple and studied at the feet of Giorgione: in the eyes of the second 'alien', this third one seemed to be the true heir to the first. Now, Tiziano and Giorgione belong to the same generation; it may even be that the student was older than the teacher. Did the two Bellinis not realize at that point that they had had their day? And what of Giovanni's true disciples? What did they say? And what did the others think, the true representatives of the school of Murano? Many of them were youths or men still young; they had all felt the influence of Antonello, but through 'Bellinismo'; the colours and light came from Messina, but Giovanni had acclimatized them; it

was through him that they had become Venetian. It was
a matter of honour to these young men to remain faith-
ful, but fidelity was stifling them; they did their best to
adapt to the new demands without abandoning the
rather crude techniques they had been taught; but this
was to condemn themselves to mediocrity. What bitterness they must have felt seeing two young interlopers
joining forces to break with local traditions, to rediscover
a Sicilian's secrets and carry painting effortlessly to the
peak of perfection? Yet Giovanni still ruled the roost;
that admirable artist's name was known throughout
northern Italy. The barbarian invasion began only in his
last years; after his death in 1516, the floodgates opened.

Now, it so happened that at the height of the invasion, the greatest painter of the century came into the
world in the heart of this occupied city, in an alleyway
on the Rialto. Dark plebeian pride, always humiliated
and repressed yet ever watchful, jumped at the occasion
and slipped into the heart of the only Rialtan who still
had talent and lifted and inflamed it. Let us remember
that he wasn't directly a child of the people, nor entirely
a scion of the bourgeoisie. His father belonged to the
comfortable artisan class. It was a point of honour for
these petty-bourgeois not to work for others: had he been
a worker's son, Jacopo would perhaps have remained the
obscure collaborator of an artist; as the son of a master
craftsman, he had to become one himself or fall in status.
He would come up through the ranks, but the honour
of his family and his class forbade him to remain in

them. One can see why he wouldn't leave a good impression in the studio where he served his apprenticeship: he entered it with the intention of leaving as soon as possible, to attain the place preordained for him in the social order. And then, what? Schiavone (or Bordone or Bonifazio dei Pitati—it matters little which) no doubt regarded him as an interloper: but Jacopo in turn regarded his master as a foreigner—in other words, as a thief. He was a *native*, this Little Dyer; Venice was his by blood. Had he been mediocre, he would have remained modest, though resentful. But he was brilliant and knew it, so he wanted to outdo everyone. In the eyes of a Rialtan, the foreigners had only their professional worth to protect them: if Jacopo did better work than them, they would have to disappear, even if it meant murdering them. No one paints or writes without a mandate to do so: would we dare to if 'I' were not 'Another?'[7] Jacopo was mandated by an entire working population to recover, by his art, the privileges of the pure-blood Venetian. This explains his clear conscience: in his heart, popular recrimination becomes an austere, assertive passion; he has been entrusted with the mission of gaining recognition for his rights; for one with such a just cause, any means of achieving it are acceptable: no quarter is given or asked. The unfortunate thing is that his struggle against the undesirables leads him to fight the patricians themselves and their assimilation policy,

---

7 A reference to Arthur Rimbaud's famous dictum, ' "Je" est un autre' ('I' is another). [Trans.]

on behalf of the indigenous artisans. When he goes down the street shouting 'Veronese to Verona!', it is the government he is challenging. As soon as he realizes this, he takes a step back and then, just as quickly, resumes his previous course. Hence this curious mixture of rigidity and flexibility: as the cautious subject of a police state, he always yields or pretends to; as the *native-born* citizen of the most beautiful of cities, his arrogance gets the better of him; he can yield to the point of servility without losing his stiff-necked pride. It is of no use: the plots he hatches against the aristocracy's protégés are either spoiled by his impatience and his irreparable acts of clumsiness or they rebound on him of their own accord. This sheds a new light on the grudge *la Serenissima* bore against him. Ultimately, he is only demanding what they would perhaps have conceded, but his quarrelsome submissiveness irritates the authorities: they see him as a rebel. Or they regard him at the very least as suspect and, in the end, they are not wrong. One has only to see what his first transport of emotion led him to.

First to that conscientious, almost sadistic violence I shall call the full employment of oneself. Born among the common people, who bear the weight of a heavily hierarchical society, he shares their tastes and fears: we can see their prudence even in his presumptuousness. His nearest and dearest, shrewd, spirited and a little cautious, taught him the price of things, instructed him in life's dangers, showed him which hopes are permitted and which forbidden. Precise and limited opportunities, a destiny marked out in advance, already legible, a future only half-open, imprisoned by transparency, a little posy of flowers too distinctly visible in the crystal of a paperweight—all these things kill dreams: you come to want only what you can have. Moderation of this kind produces madmen and gives rise to the fiercest ambitions, though short-term ones. Jacopo's ambition sprang into being all of a sudden, already booted and helmeted, with its particular virulence and forms; it is identical with that slim shaft of light, the possible. Or, rather, nothing is *possible*: there is the end and the means, the prescribed task. One will raise oneself above the heaviest, lowest clouds, one will touch a taut, luminous skin with one hand—this is the ceiling. There are other ceilings, clearer and clearer membranes, thinner and thinner ones. And perhaps, way up at the top, there's the blue of the sky. But Tintoretto couldn't give a damn about that; everyone has his own upward force and his natural resting place. He knows he is gifted; he has been told it is a form of capital. If he proves his ability, he will have a profitable enterprise to his name and will find the funds to equip it. He is set on his way with a long lifetime ahead; his time is already spoken for: there is this seam to be mined and he will do so until both seam and miner are exhausted. Around the same time, that other glutton for work, Michelangelo, turns his nose up at the opportunity; he begins the work and runs off without finishing it. Tintoretto *always* finishes his work, with the fearsome application of a man who always finishes his sentences, come what may. Death itself waited for him at San Giorgio, it let him apply the last brushstroke to the last painting or, at least, give the last instructions to his collaborators. He never in the whole of his life permitted himself a whim, a moment's distaste or a preference; not even the luxury of a dream. He must have repeated this watchword to himself on his tired days: to turn down a commission is to make a present to the competition.

One has to produce at all costs. On this point, the will of one man and that of a city are in agreement. A hundred years earlier, Donatello criticized Uccello for sacrificing creation to research and carrying the love of painting to the point of no longer producing pictures. But that was in Florence: Florentine artists had just launched themselves into the hazardous adventure of *perspective*; they were trying to construct a new plastic space by applying the laws of geometric optics to painted objects. *Autres temps, autres moeurs.* At Venice, with Titian reigning supreme, everyone was of the view that painting had just achieved the height of perfection, that there was simply no further to go: art is dead, long live life. The great barbarism begins with Aretino's foolish remarks 'How lifelike it is! How true it is! *You'd never think it was painted*!' In short, it was time for painting to take a back seat to *positive creations*: the inspired merchants wanted useful beauty. The art work must give pleasure to the *amateur*, bear witness before Europe to Venice's most serene splendour and strike awe into the populace. The awe has lasted to this day: when faced with Venetian cinemascope, we humble tourists mutter: 'It's directed by Titian, it's a Veronese production, it's a performance by Pordenone, a staging by Vicentino.' Jacopo Robusti shares the prejudices of his age and our smart observers hold that against him. How many times have I heard it said, 'Tintoretto—mere theatrics!' And yet no one in the world, either before or after, has taken the passion for experimentation further. With Titian, painting flowers to the point of suffocation; it negates itself by its own perfection. Jacopo sees this death as the necessary precondition for a resurrection: everything is beginning, everything remains to be done; we shall come back to this. But—and here is his major contradiction—he will never tolerate his experiments restricting his productivity. Were there only a single wall left in Venice unpainted, the artist's duty is to paint it: morality forbids one to turn a studio into a laboratory. Art is both a serious profession and a bitter struggle against the invaders. Like Titian, like Veronese, Jacopo will serve up exquisite corpses. With one difference: these dead bodies have a feverishness about them that might be a revival of life or the beginnings of decay. And if he absolutely has to be compared to our film directors, it is *in this respect* that he is like them: he takes on mindless scenarios and then subtly loads his own obsessions on to them. One must fool the buyer, give him more than his money's worth: he will have his Catherine, Teresa or Sebastian; and for the same price he can be in the picture, and with his wife or brothers if he insists. But underneath, behind the sumptuous, banal facade of this *creation*, Tintoretto carries on with his experimentation. All his major works have a double meaning: his narrow utilitarianism masks an endless questioning. In setting his research within the framework of the paid commission, he is forced to revolutionize painting while at the same time respecting the client's stipulations. This is the deep-seated reason for his overwork; it will later be the reason for his downfall.

And yet he still had to corner the market. We have seen that he worked at this. But if we go back, now, over his methods, they will show up in a fresh light. Tintoretto's rebellion becomes more radical: in revolt against the 'melting-pot' policy, he is forced to infringe guild rules or customs. Unable to eliminate competition, the advantages of which they do in fact acknowledge, the government strive to channel it through formal contests. If it is their taste that decides in the last instance, the rich and powerful will preserve public order and establish that flexible form of protectionism that is 'managed competition'. Are they sincere? Without a doubt, and everything would be perfect if we had proof of their capacities. But we have to take their word on that score. It does happen that they make the right choice, but at other times, they opt for Vicentino. For his part, Tintoretto always manages to escape the test. Is it because he denies them any competence? Absolutely not: he simply feels they have no right to treat a native-born Venetian on the same footing as interlopers.

The fact remains that these contests exist: by avoiding them, our rebel is deliberately seeking to destroy protectionism. He is in a corner: since the authorities claim to judge on the basis of value, and since he rejects their judgement, he has either to give up painting or to make his reputation by the quality of his painting. That is no problem; he finds other ways, pips his competitors to the post and presents the judges with a *fait accompli*; he deploys his skill, his speed and his collaborators' diligence to achieve a level of mass production that puts a bomb under all the price scales, allowing him to sell his canvases for paltry sums—or even give them away. There is an avenue in Rome with two cheap clothes shops on opposite sides of the street; the shopkeepers have, I imagine, come to some agreement to simulate a fight to the death—unless the two establishments are owned by the same person, a tragic actor, who enjoys eternally pitting the two aspects of his nature against each other. On the one side, there is a window criss-crossed with funereal notices: *Prezzi disastrosi*! On the other, little multi-coloured posters announce: *Prezzi da ridere! da ridere! da ridere!* This has been going on for years and I can never pass these shops without being reminded of Tintoretto. Did he choose to laugh or cry? Both, in my view, depending on the client. We may even suppose that he sniggered a little in solitude, and that he lamented when he was among his family, complaining that he was being bled dry. All the same, it was 'sale time' all year round in his studio, and his clients felt the lure of these clearance prices. Having started out to commission a tiny inset portrait, they ended up giving him every wall in the house to paint. He was the first to break the already crumbling bonds of guild brotherhood: for this pre-Darwinian Darwinist, fellow guild members became his closest enemies. He beat Hobbes to the slogan of absolute competition: *Homo homini lupus*. Venice was roused to indignation. If a vaccine couldn't be found against the Tintoretto virus, he would dissolve corporate good order and leave only a cloud of antagonisms and molecular solitudes. The Republic condemned these new methods, called them felonies, spoke of botched work, undercutting, monopoly practices. Later—much later—other cities, in another language, would honour these methods as 'the struggle for life' or as 'mass production', would speak of 'dumping' or 'monopoly practices', etc. For the moment, this notorious character lost on the swings everything he had gained on the roundabouts. He won commissions at bayonet point, but socially he was shunned. In a strange turnabout, he, the *native*, the hundred per cent Rialtan, was the one who seemed an interloper—and almost an undesirable—in his own city.

The inevitable consequence is that he will perish if he doesn't start a family. First, to stifle competition from within his studio: this champion of free markets reverses the biblical precept; he makes sure others can never do unto him as has done unto them. And then, he needs total approval; outsiders working with him might be frightened off or discouraged by the vague sense of scandal around him; how much time he might waste stiffening their resolve. From now on, this thunder will release only damp squibs of lightning. What need has he of disciples? He wants other hands, other pairs of arms and that is all. Through absolute competition to family-based enterprise: this is the path. In 1550, he marries Faustina dei Vescovi and, there and then, begins producing children. Doing so the way he produces pictures—with indefatigable bolts of thunder. And this excellent child-bearer has only one failing: she overdoes the daughters somewhat. Never mind, he will put them all in a convent, except for two: Marietta, whom he keeps by him, and Ottavia, whom he marries off to a painter. The thunder will fecundate Faustina as many times as necessary to get two sons from her, Domenico and Marco. But he didn't wait for them to come along before he taught the trade to his eldest daughter, Marietta. A woman painter in Venice is no everyday affair: what a hurry he must have been in! Finally, around 1575, it was mission accomplished: the new personnel consisted of his son-in-law Sebastian Casser, Marietta, Domenico and Marco. The symbol of a domestic association is the *domus* that shelters and imprisons it. At around this same date, Jacopo bought a house. He would spend the rest of his days there. In this little *lazaretto*, the leper would live in semi-quarantine amid his family, loving them all the more, the more *others* there were to detest him. Seen *in the home*, in his work, in his relations with his wife and children, we find quite a different side to him: what a stern

moralist! And a little Calvinistic round the edges perhaps? He had all the attributes: pessimism and work, the
spirit of lucre and devotion to his family. Human nature
is marred by original sin; men are divided by their interests. The Christian will be saved by works: let him battle
against all; let him labour unremittingly, being hard on
himself and on others, to embellish the Earth God has
entrusted to him; he will find the mark of divine favour
in the material success of his enterprise. As for the stir-
rings of his heart, let him keep them for the flesh of his
flesh: his sons. Did Venice feel the influence of the
reformed religion? It certainly did. In the second half of
the century we find there a curious individual, Fra Paolo
Sarpi. He has the ear of the patricians, is a friend of
Galileo's, is hostile to Rome and openly maintains close
ties with foreign Protestant circles. But if, in some intellectual circles, we can detect tendencies vaguely sympa-
thetic to the Reformation, it is more than probable that
the petty-bourgeoisie knew nothing of them. It would
be more accurate to say that *la Serenissima* reformed
itself. And this reformation had been going on a long
time: Venice's merchants lived from credit; they could
not accept the Church's condemnation of those it
insisted on calling usurers; they encouraged science when
it brought practical benefits and scorned Roman obscu-
rantism. The Venetian state had always affirmed the
precedence of the civil authorities; that was its doctrine;
it would not change it. In practical terms, it was the state
that had control of its clergy, and, when Pius V took it

into his head to remove ecclesiastics from lay jurisdiction, the Senate rejected the move outright. And for many reasons the government regarded the Holy See more as a temporal, military power than a spiritual one. Though this did not prevent it, when the interests of the Republic were at stake, from cosying up to the Pope, hunting out heretics or, to please the Very Christian Monarch, organizing a sumptuous celebration in honour of Saint-Bartholomew. Tintoretto took his pseudo-Calvinism from his city itself: unwittingly, the painter tapped into the latent Protestantism one finds at the time in all the great capitalist cities.[8] The status of artists was particularly ambivalent in this period, especially in Venice. But let us try our luck; perhaps this very ambiguity will enable us to understand Jacopo's dark puritanical passion.

Vuillemin has argued that 'the Renaissance [had] lent artists the features that Antiquity reserved for men of action and with which the Middle Ages adorned its saints.'[9] This is not wrong. But the opposite seems to me at least as true: '[In the sixteenth century] painting and sculpture were still regarded as manual arts; all honour was reserved for poetry. Hence the efforts made by the figurative arts to compete with literature.'[10] There can

8 That latent Protestantism that inoculates Italian cities against the Lutheran disease and leads Italy to carry out its own religious revolution under the name of the Counter-Reformation.

9 Jules Vuillemin, 'La personnalité esthétique du Tintoret', *Les Temps modernes*, 102 (1954).

10 These are the words of Eugenio Battista in an excellent article on Michaelangelo—'Michaelangelo: credeva nell'arte ma disperava

be no doubt, in fact, that Aretino, that poor man's Petronius, that rich man's Malaparte, was the arbiter of taste and elegance for the bright young things of the Venetian patriciate, nor that Titian prided himself on being one of his circle: all Titian's fame was barely enough to make him the equal of Aretino. And Michelangelo? His weakness was the belief that he was a naturally patrician soul and this illusion ruined his life. As a very young man, he would have liked to have studied the classics and written: a man of the lesser nobility may take up the pen without losing status. He took up the chisel out of necessity and never got over it. Michelangelo looked down on sculpture and painting from the pinnacle of his shame; he had the awkward, empty joy of feeling superior to his occupation. Forced into silence, he attempted to give a language to the dumb arts, to create a profusion of allegories and symbols; he wrote a book on the ceiling of the Sistine chapel and he tortured marble to compel it to speak.

What conclusions are we to draw? Were the painters of the Renaissance demigods or manual labourers? Well, it just depends: it depends on the clients and the method of remuneration. Or, rather, they were manual workers *first*. After that, they became employees of the court or remained local masters. It was up to them to choose— or be chosen. Raphael and Michelangelo were agents of the state; they lived haughtily but in a condition of

---

della sorte dell'uomo'—published by *Epoca* 8(360) (25 August 1957): 35–50.

dependence. Even a temporary fall from grace could put them on the street; on the other hand, the sovereign took care of their publicity. That sacred personage yielded a portion of his supernatural powers to his chosen ones: the glory of the throne fell on them like a ray of sunlight and they reflected it on to the people; the divine right of kings produced divine-right painters. With it, mere daubers were changed into supermen. And what were they, in fact, these petty-bourgeois whom a giant hand had plucked from the crowd and suspended between heaven and earth—these satellites who dazzled with a borrowed brilliance—but human beings raised above humanity? Heroes they were indeed: that is to say, they were intercessors, intermediaries. Even today, when they employ the word 'genius', nostalgic republicans still worship, through them, the light of that dead star, monarchy.

Tintoretto was a member of the other species: he worked for merchants, civil servants and parish churches. I am not saying he was uneducated: he was sent to school at seven and must have left it at twelve knowing how to read and count. And, most importantly, how could one not term 'education' that patient training of senses, hand and mind, that traditionalist practice of trial and error, which studio painting still represented in the years around 1530. But he would never have the cultural baggage of the court painters. Michelangelo wrote sonnets; it is said today that Raphael knew Latin; and the frequenting of intellectuals eventually gave Titian himself a veneer of refinement. Compared with these fashionable men, Tintoretto seems unlettered: he would never have the taste and leisure to engage in the life of ideas or the world of letters. He didn't give a fig for the humanism of the literate classes. Venice had few poets and even fewer philosophers: in his view, that was already too many and he didn't mix with any. Not that he avoided them: he simply knew nothing of them. He accepted their social superiority. Aretino had the right to congratulate him with protective benevolence: that lofty personage was *admitted to society*; he was part of fashionable Venice; he was invited to dinner by patricians who would not even greet a painter in the street. But did he have to envy him into the bargain? Did he have to envy him *because he was a writer*? Jacopo felt that the works of the mind had a highly immoral air of gratuitousness about them: God put us on the Earth to gain our daily bread by the sweat of our brow, but writers do not sweat. Do they even work? Jacopo never opened a book, with the exception of his missal; the bizarre idea of stretching his talent to compete with literature was not one that would have occurred to him: there is everything in his pictures, but they have *no message to deliver*; they are silent as the world itself. Ultimately, this craftsman's son respected only physical effort and manual creation. What enchanted him in the painting profession was the fact that occupational skill was taken to the point of prestidigitation, and the refinement of the product to the point of quintessence. The artist was, for him, the supreme worker: he tired himself out and exhausted matter in order to produce and sell visions. This would not prevent him working for princes if he liked them. But when all was said and done, he didn't like them: they frightened him without inspiring him. He never tried to approach them or to make himself known: one might say he made every effort to restrict his fame to within the walls of Venice. It is not perhaps well-known that he never left the city, except once, in his sixties, to travel to nearby Mantua. Even then, he had to be begged to do so: they wanted him to hang his paintings himself and he was adamant he would not go unless he could take his wife with him. The demand attests, in part, to his strong conjugal feelings, but it says much, too, about his dread of travel. And we should not be deceived into thinking his Venetian colleagues shared the same aversion; they went gallivanting off in all directions. And a hundred years earlier Gentile Bellini did so by sea. What adventurers they were! He, by contrast, was a mole: he was at ease only in the narrow tunnels of his molehill. If he imagined the world, agoraphobia laid him low; yet, if he had to choose, he would still rather endanger himself than his paintings. He accepted commissions from abroad—and 'abroad' for him began at Padua— but he didn't go looking for them. What a contrast between this indifference and his passionate pursuit of work at the Doges' Palace, at the Scuola San Rocco and from the *Crociferi*! He entrusted the execution of these other works to his collaborators, overseeing these mass productions from a distance, refraining from putting his own hand to them, as though he feared for the tiniest scintilla of his talent to go outside his homeland: Europe would get only his 'B Pictures'. You can find Raphael, Titian and a hundred others at the Uffizi, the Prado, the National Gallery, the Louvre and in Munich or Vienna. All of them, or almost all, but not Tintoretto. He kept himself fiercely for his fellow-citizens and you will know nothing of him unless you go and look for him in his native city, for the very good reason that he didn't *wish* to leave it.

But we must clarify this point, for in Venice itself he had two very different clienteles. He laid siege to the public officials and, naturally, if the Senate gave him work, the whole of the studio got involved, including the head of the household. At the Doges' Palace, in lighting that shows them to advantage, you can still see the works of a strong collective personality bearing the name of Tintoretto. But if it's Jacopo Robusti who interests you, then leave the Piazzetta behind, walk across the Piazza San Marco, take the humpbacked bridges over the canals and wander around in a labyrinth of dark alleyways where there are still darker churches for you to enter. And there he is. In the Scuola San Rocco you have him—in person, without Marietta, Domenico or Sebastiano Casser. He worked there alone. These canvases are shrouded in a dirty mist, or reflections make it difficult to see them properly. Wait patiently till your eyes get used to the light: you will in the end see a rose in the shadows, a guardian spirit in the semi-darkness. And who paid for these paintings? Sometimes it was the church's congregation, sometimes the members of the Brotherhood: big and petty bourgeois. They were his real audience, the only one he loved.

There was nothing of the demigod about this commercial painter. With a little luck, he would be notorious, famous, but he would never gain genuine glory: his clientele of outsiders did not have the power to hallow him in that way. Of course, the renown of his august colleagues reflected on the whole of the profession and he shone a little too. Did he envy them their glory? Perhaps. But he did nothing of what would have been needed to acquire it. The favour of princes could go hang: it was something that enslaved you. Jacopo Robusti took pride in remaining a small master, a small trader in the Fine Arts, paid by the job, but in command of his own establishment. He made no distinction between the economic independence of the producer and the freedom of the artist. His scheming proves that he hoped somehow to revolutionize market conditions, to promote demand through supply: among the members of the Brotherhood of San Rocco did he not slowly and patiently create a need for art—for a certain art—that only he could satisfy? His autonomy was all the better preserved by the fact of working for collective bodies—such as consorteries or parishes—and by their taking their decisions by majority vote.

That false aristocrat Michelangelo and that son of the soil Titian felt the attraction of monarchy directly. Tintoretto was born in a milieu of self-employed workers. The craftsman is an amphibian: as a manual worker, he is proud of his hands; as a petty-bourgeois, the upper bourgeoisie exerts an attraction: it was that class which, by the mere play of competition, enabled some air to penetrate into a stifling protectionist system. There was in those days *hope for the bourgeoisie* in Venice. It was a slim hope; the aristocracy had long since taken its precautions: in that stratified universe, you could *become* rich but you had to *be born* a patrician. But even wealth was limited: not only did the trader or industrialist remain confined to their class, but the most lucrative occupations had long been closed to them; the State granted the *appalto*—the hiring of galleys—to aristocrats alone. Sombre and dreamy bourgeoisie![11] Everywhere else, in Europe, the middle classes were turning against their own past—buying up titles and castles as quickly as they could. In Venice, they were denied everything, even the lowly pleasure of betrayal. They would, then, betray in imagination. Arriving from Piacenza, Giovita Fontana launched herself into business, earned a fortune and spent it on a *palazza* on the Canale Grande. There is an entire existence in these few words: a fierce desire, once satisfied, turns in latter years into snobbish reverie; a merchantess dies and is reborn as an imaginary patrician. The rich

---

11 There is an allusion here to Pierre Drieu la Rochelle's novel of 1937, *Rêveuse bourgeoisie* (Paris: Gallimard, 1937). [Trans.]

commoners thrashed around, hiding away their nocturnal fantasies. Grouped into confraternities, they consumed their energies in charitable works, their melancholy austerity contrasting with the melancholy orgies of a disenchanted patriciate.

For the Republic no longer ruled the seas. The aristocracy gradually began to decline, the bankruptcy rate increased, the ranks of the impoverished nobility swelled, while the other nobles lost the spirit of enterprise: these sons of ship-owners bought up land, became *rentiers*. Mere 'citizens' were already replacing them in certain functions: the galleys fell under the command of the bourgeois. The bourgeoisie was still far from regarding itself as a rising class; it didn't even dare to believe it could one day take over from the fallen nobility: let us say, rather, that it was seized by an obscure agitation that rendered its condition less bearable and made a resigned attitude more difficult.

Tintoretto didn't dream. Never. If people's ambitions are geared to the openness of their social horizons, then the most ambitious commoners in Venice were the petty-bourgeois, since they still had a chance of rising out of their class. But the painter felt deep affinities with his customers; he appreciated their commitment to hard work, their moralism, their practicality. He liked their nostalgia and, above all, he shared their deepest aspiration: they all, if only to produce, to buy and to sell, had need of freedom. These are the clues to his *arrivisme*: he was drawn on by an up-draught from the heights. Disturbances in the heavens, a distant, invisible ascent opened up a vertical future; he climbed, this Cartesian diver; with the new spirit in him, a draught of fresh air drew him upwards: since childhood he had thought like a bourgeois. But the contradictions of his class of origin were to limit his ambitions: as a small trader, he hoped to cross the line; as a 'worker', he sought to work with his hands. That was enough to mark out his place. There were—approximately—7,600 patricians in Venice, 13,600 citizens, 127,000 artisans, workers and small traders, 1,500 Israelites, 12,900 servants and 550 beggars. Leaving aside Jews, nobles, beggars and servants, Tintoretto focussed exclusively on the ideal demarcation line that divided the commoners into two groups: 13,600 on one side, 127,000 on the other. He wanted to be the first among the latter and the last among the former: in a word, the humblest of the rich and the most distinguished among the purveyors to the rich. In the heart of troubled Venice, that made this artisan a false bourgeois who was more genuine than the genuine article. What the Brotherhood of San Rocco would love in him and his paintings would be the beautified image of a bourgeoisie that was not disloyal.

Even when working for the Supreme Pontiff, Michelangelo would think he was demeaning himself. That contempt sometimes afforded him a critical distance: this nobleman had some cavalier ideas on art. Tintoretto was entirely the opposite; he operated at a level beyond that of his birth. Without art, what would he be? A dyer. It was his own strength that had lifted him out of his native condition and what kept him at that level was his dignity. He had to work or fall back to the bottom of the pile. Objectivity? Critical distance? Where would he acquire such things? He hadn't the time to examine his thoughts about painting? Who knows if he even *saw* it? Michelangelo thought too much: he was a Marquis de Carabas, an intellectual. Tintoretto didn't know what he was doing: he painted.

So much for his *arrivisme*: the destiny of this artist was to embody bourgeois Puritanism in a declining aristocratic Republic. In other places, this sombre humanism was the order of the day; at Venice, it would disappear without even having become conscious of itself, though not without arousing the distrust of an ever watchful aristocracy. The surliness that official, bureaucratic Venice society displayed towards Tintoretto was the same surliness the patriciate showed towards the Venetian bourgeoisie. These quarrelsome merchants and their painter represented a danger to the order of *La Serenissima*: an eye had to be kept on them.

The Hunted Man

One may find a degree of disdainful pride in the stubborn refusal to compete: 'I know of no one to rival me and I accept no judge.' Michelangelo would perhaps have said that. The unfortunate thing is that Tintoretto did not. On the contrary, if he were invited to submit a sketch, he would rush to comply. After that, we know he flung his thunderbolts. More or less in the way a squid squirts out its ink. Lighting bolts have a blinding effect and the spectators weren't able to make out his painting. And, indeed, everything was arranged so that they never needed to view it, nor, particularly, evaluate it. When the dazzle had dissipated, the canvas was hung and the gift recorded. They had been completely hoodwinked. Either I am very much mistaken or this is an evasion on his part; it seems as though he was afraid to confront his adversaries. Would he go to such ingenious lengths if he were confident that his talent would win out? Would he deign to astonish his contemporaries with the quantity of his output if they unreservedly admired its quality?

And then this passion for asserting himself through suppressing his own personality was even more striking in competitions. But it was his style, his trademark: the slightest comparison offended his sensibilities; being set alongside others troubled him. In 1559, the Church of San Rocco commissioned from him *The Impotent Man at the Pool of Bethesda* to go alongside a Pordenone. No one asked him to imitate the style of his predecessor and there could be no competition between the two.[12] Antonio de' Sacchis[13] had been dead for twenty years. If he could in the past have influenced the younger man, the time for influences was over: Jacopo was now the master of his art. Yet, the urge was too strong to resist: he had to 'do' a Pordenone. A very good account has been given of how he 'exaggerated the baroque violence of gestures . . . by the clash between the monumental figures and the architecture into which they were intimately inserted' and how he 'achieved this effect by lowering the ceiling of the hall . . . by [using] the columns themselves . . . [to] arrest the gestures and freeze their violence'.[14]

---

12 Ridolfi, deceived by the stylistic resemblance, said the picture was painted 'in concorrenza con il Pordenone' [in competition with Pordenone—Trans.].

13 Giovanni Antionio de' Sacchis was the actual name of the painter known as Pordenone. [Trans.]

14 Vuillemin, *op cit.*, p. 1974. See also Tietze, p. 372, Newton, p. 72. [These are probably references to the following editions: H. Tietze, *Tintoretto: The Paintings and Drawings* (London: Phaidon

In short, he trembled at the idea of being eternally imprisoned in an inert face-off: 'Compare, if you will, the Pordenone with the Pordenone; I, Jacopo Robusti, am not here.' He contrived, of course, that the false de Sacchis would crush the genuine one. His withdrawal was no rout: he departed with a defiant shout on his lips: 'I take them all on, ancients and moderns, and defeat them on their own home ground.' But here precisely lies the element that will seem suspect: why does he need to play their game, to submit to their rules, when he would only have to be himself to crush them? What resentment there is in his insolence: he is a Cain murdering all the Abels who are preferred to him: 'You like Veronese? Well, when I deign to imitate him, I can do better; you see him as a man, but he is merely a method.' What humility too: from time to time, this outcast slips into the skin of another to experience, in his turn, the sweetness of being loved. And then sometimes you'd think the courage to display his scandalous genius had deserted him; weary of the struggle, he leaves it in the semi-darkness and attempts to prove it by *reductio ad absurdum*: 'Since I paint the best Veroneses and the best Pordenones, just imagine *what I can do* when I consent to be myself.' In fact, he very rarely gave himself such consent, unless he was shown total trust from the start and left quite alone in an empty room. The origin of this lay, of course, in the hostility displayed towards him. But the painter's

Press, 1948); Eric Newton, *Tintoretto* (London: Longmans, Green and Co., 1952)—Trans.]

timidity and the bias of his fellow-citizens both originated in the same disturbing moment: in 1584, at Venice, at the hand of Tintoretto and before the patricians, art-lovers and aesthetes, *painting gave itself a fright.*

A long process of development began here and it was everywhere to substitute the profane for the sacred: cold, sparkling and frosty, the various branches of human activity will emerge one after the other from their sweet intermingling in the divine. Art was affected: out of a bank of mist emerged the sumptuous disenchantment that was painting. It still remembered the time when Duccio or Giotto showed God the Creation exactly as it had left His hands: as soon as He had recognized His works, the affair was in the bag and the world was, for all eternity, in a frame. Between the picture—the realm of the Sun—and the supreme Eye, monks and prelates would sometimes interpose their transparent forms; they would come on tiptoe to see what God Himself saw, and then they would excuse themselves and leave. It was over: the Eye was closed, the Heavens blind. So what happened? First, there was a change of clientele: so long as one was working for clerics, all was well; the day the biggest of the Florentine bankers formed the curious notion of decking out his house with frescoes, the Almighty retreated, sickened, into his role as Lover of Souls. And then there was the great Florentine adventure: the conquest of perspective. Perspective is a profane thing—sometimes, even, a profanation. Take Mantegna's

Christ, painted lengthways, his feet in the foreground and his head at the back of beyond. Do you think the Father could be happy with a foreshortened Son? God is absolute proximity, the universal embrace of Love: can one take the universe that He made—and that He constantly preserves from annihilation—and show it to Him *from a distance*? Is it for Beings to conceive and produce Non-Being? Is it for the Absolute to engender the Relative? Is it right that Light should contemplate Shade? That Reality should take itself for Appearance? No, this is the eternal story beginning again: Innocence, the Tree of Knowledge, Original Sin and the Casting-out from the Garden. Only, this time, the apple is called 'perspective'. But the Adamites of Florence merely nibble at it rather than eating, which prevents them from learning immediately of their Fall: in mid-Quattrocento, Uccello still believes himself to be in Paradise, and poor old Alberti, the theorist of the 'perspectivists', is still presenting Geometric Optics as an Ontology of Visibility. When all is said and done, he remains so guileless as to demand of the divine Gaze that it approve perspective's 'lines of flight'. To this absurd request Heaven remained silent: the creature was smartly consigned to that nothingness which is properly his own and which he had just rediscovered. Distance, banishment, separation—these negations mark our limits; only man has a horizon. Alberti's window opens on to a measurable universe, but that rigorous miniature depends entirely on the point that defines our anchorage and dispersal: namely, on our eyes. In his Annunciation, between the Angel and the Virgin, Piero della Francesca shows us an unfathomable arrangement of columns: this is an appearance; in themselves and for their Creator, these inert masses of white, each the same and each incomparable, continue their slumber: perspective is a violence human weakness inflicts on God's little world. A hundred years later in the Netherlands, they will rediscover the Being in the depths of Appearing and appearance will recover its dignity as emergence: painting will have new aims; it will find a new meaning. But, before Vermeer can give us the sky, the stars, day and night, the moon and the earth in the form of a little wall of bricks, the burghers of the North will have to win their greatest victories and forge their humanism.

In Italy in the sixteenth century, artists' hearts are still aglow with faith; that faith combats the atheism of the eye and the hand. Through wishing to cleave ever more keenly to the Absolute, they have developed techniques that throw them into a relativism they detest. Mystified dogmatists that they are, they can neither press forward nor go back. If God no longer looks at the pictures they paint, who will bear witness for them? They reflect man's powerlessness back to him: where will he find the strength to stand surety for them? And then, if painting's only purpose is to gauge the extent of our short-sightedness, it isn't worth an hour's trouble. Showing man to the Almighty, who deigned to raise him from the mire, was an act of thanksgiving, a sacrifice. But why would you show him to Man? Why show him *as he is not*? The artists of the end of the century—those born around 1480: Titian, Raphael and Giorgione—reached an accommodation with Heaven. We shall come back to this. And then the wealth and effectiveness of means still concealed the baleful indeterminacy of ends. We may presume Raphael had some premonition of this: he didn't give a damn for anything; chased after loose women, sold cheap prints, and, out of *Schadenfreude*, encouraged his collaborators to make obscene etchings: his was a suicide by facility. In any event, the joy of painting disappears with these legendary figures. In the second quarter of the century, painting runs wild, led astray by its own perfection. In the barbarous taste contemporaries affected for great *realizzazioni*, we can discern an unease: the public calls for all the splendours of realism to be used to conceal one's subjectivity; for the author of the work to efface himself before life itself, to let himself be forgotten. The desirable thing would be to come across paintings unawares, on the edge of a wood, and for the characters in them to tear themselves from the canvas and, in a shower of broken fragments of picture frame, to jump at the throats of passers-by. The object should reabsorb its visibility, should contain it within itself, should deflect attention from it by a continuous appeal to all the senses and, in particular, to touch. Everything should be done to replace *representation* by an implicit participation of the spectator in the spectacle; horror and tenderness should throw men up against their simulacra and, if possible, in the midst of these, desire, cutting through all restrictions of perspective, should discover that *ersatz* of divine ubiquity: the immediate presence of the flesh. The Reason of the eye should be respected, and yet it should be combated by the reasons of the heart. What was wanted was *the thing itself,* and that it should be a crushing presence; that it should be bigger than nature, more present and more beautiful. Such a desire is a desire for Terror. But Terror is a sickness of Rhetoric. Art, ashamed, will seek to hide itself once it has lost its letters of credit. Tied down now under the surveillance and restrictions of State, Church and taste, the artist, though beset perhaps with more attention and honour than ever before, for the first time in history becomes aware of his solitude. Who gave him his mandate? Whence does this entitlement he claims for himself derive? It is Night, and God has expired: how is one to paint in the darkness? And for *whom*? And *what*? And *why*? Art's object remains *the world*, that absolute: but reality is giving way, and the relation of the finite to the infinite has been overturned. The wretchedness of bodies and their fragility had been sustained by an immense plenitude. Now, fragility is becoming the only plenitude, the only security: the Infinite is the void, the blackness both within creatures and outside them. The Absolute is absence, it is God having taken refuge in souls: it is the desert. It is too late to *show*, too late to *create*; the painter is in hell; something is being born, a new damnation: genius—that uncertainty, that insane

desire to pass beyond the Night of the world and contemplate it from the outside and crush it on to the walls,
on to the canvases, bathing it in a previously unknown
light. Genius, a new word in Europe, a conflict between
the relative and the absolute, between a limited presence
and an infinite absence. For the painter well knows he
will never leave the world behind. And then, even if he
were to, he would take with him everywhere this nothingness that runs through him: one cannot transcend
perspective until one has granted oneself the right to create other plastic spaces.

Michelangelo dies a haunted man, summing up his
despair and contempt in two words: original sin. Tintoretto says nothing; he cheats: were he to admit his
loneliness to himself, he would not be able to bear it.
But, for this very reason, we can understand that he suf-
fers from it more than anyone: this false bourgeois working for the bourgeois does not even have the excuse of
fame. This is the nest of vipers: a little dyer quivers,
afflicted with that character neurosis Henri Jeanson so
aptly terms 'the terrifying moral health of the ambitious';
he sets himself modest goals: to raise himself above his
father by the judicious exploitation of his gifts, to dom-
inate the market by flattering public taste. Cheerful
arrivisme, ability, speed and talent—he lacks nothing,
yet all is gnawed at by a dizzying absence, by Art without
God. That Art is ugly, wicked, nocturnal; it is the mindless passion of the part for the whole, a wind of ice and
darkness howling through pierced hearts. Sucked

towards the Void, Jacopo is swallowed up by a journey that goes nowhere, and from which he will never return.

Genius doesn't exist: it is the shameful audacity of the nothingness. The little dyer does exist and he knows his limitations: this sensible boy wants to repair the tear in the fabric. All he asks is a modest fullness: what does he care for the infinite? And how would he admit to himself that the tiniest brushstroke is enough to challenge the competence of his judges. His stubborn, petty ambition would unravel in the Night of Unknowing. It isn't his fault, after all, if painting is a stray dog with no collar:[15] later, there will be madmen who will rejoice in their abandonment; in the middle of the sixteenth century, the first victim of monocular perspective was concerned, first of all, to conceal his own. Working alone and to no end was a terrifying thing. He needed judges. At any price. A panel of judges. God was silent; that left Venice: Venice which stopped up the gaps, filled in the holes, blocked up the outlets, stopped the haemorrhaging and the leaks. In the Republic of the Doges, good subjects were answerable to the state for all their activities; if it happened that they painted, they did so for the adornment of the city. Jacopo put himself into the hands of his fellow citizens; they had a certain, highly academic conception of Art, which he rapidly adopted. All the

---

15 This phrase clearly echoes the title of Gilbert Cesbron's *Chiens perdus sans collier*, a bestseller on the theme of juvenile delinquency in which the central character is an orphan. Cesbron's novel appeared in 1954, three years before this essay. [Trans.]

more rapidly for the fact that it had always been his own. Since his earliest childhood, he had been told—and had believed—that a craftsman's worth is measured by the number and size of the commissions he receives and the honours paid to him. He would hide his genius behind his *arrivisme* and take social success as the only clear sign of mystical victory. His bad faith was patent to the blindest; on earth, he played his hand of cards and cheated; and then there was the dice-throw against heaven, in which he didn't cheat. Now if he wins in this world, with all the aces he pulls from his sleeve, he dares to claim he will have won in heaven; if he sells his canvases, it is because he will have caught the world in his trap. But who could hold this great mischief against him? It was the nineteenth century that declared the divorce between the artist and the public. In the sixteenth, it is *true* that painting was going mad: it had ceased to be a religious sacrifice. But it is *no less true,* that it was becoming more rational: it remained a service performed for society. Who in Venice would dare, then, to say. 'I paint for myself, I am my own witness?' And are we sure that those who say this today are not lying? Everyone is a judge and no one is: make of that what you can. Tintoretto seems more unfortunate than guilty: his art rends the age with a fiery dart, but he can see it only with the eyes of his times. The fact remains that he has chosen his own hell: at a single stroke the finite closes on the infinite, ambition upon genius and Venice on its painter, who will never again leave it. But the captive infinite gnaws away at everything: Jacopo's reasonable *arrivisme* becomes a frenzy; it had merely been a matter of rising in society; now he must *prove* something. Having voluntarily placed himself in the position of defendant, the unfortunate man has become embroiled in an endless trial. He will mount his own defence, making each picture a witness in his own cause and never ceasing to plead his case: there is the city of Venice to convince, with its magistrates and burghers who, alone and with no possibility of appeal, will decide on his mortal future and his immortality. Now, he and he alone brought about this strange conflation. He had to choose: he could either rely on himself alone and legislate without appeal to anyone else or transform the Most Serene Republic into an absolute tribunal. Having said this, he took the only option he could—to his great misfortune. But how well I understand the indifference he felt towards the rest of the universe! What need did he have of German or even Florentine support? Venice is the finest, richest city; it has the best painters and critics, the most enlightened art lovers: it is *here* the game has to be played, with every move an irrevocable one; *here* in a brick corridor between a thin strip of sky and the stagnant waters, beneath the blazing absence of the sun, Eternity will be won or lost in a single life, forever.

All well and good, you may say, but why cheat? Why put on Veronese's fine plumage? If he wants to dazzle them with his genius, why snuff it out so often? And why apportion judges for himself if it is only to corrupt and deceive them?

Why? Because the tribunal is biased, the cause lost, the sentence passed and because he knows it. In 1548, he asks Venice to sanction the infinite; it takes fright and refuses. What a destiny! Abandoned by God, he has to cheat to find himself judges; having found them, it takes further skulduggery to get the trial adjourned. He will spend his life keeping them in suspense, at times running away, at others turning round to blind them. It is all here: the pain and the anger, the arrogance, the pliability, the furious effort, the rancour, the unbending pride and the humble desire to be loved. Tintoretto's painting is, above all else, the love affair between a man and a city.

A Mole in the Sun

In this tale of madness, the city seems even madder than the man. Since she managed to honour all her painters, why display such sourness, such sullen distrust towards the greatest of them all? Well, quite simply because she loves another. *La Serenissima* is hungry for prestige: her fame was for many years assured by her ships. Weary now and having gone down in the world a little, she vested her pride in an artist. Titian was worth a whole fleet by himself: stealing brilliance from the gleaming crowns and tiaras, he had wreathed himself in it. His adopted country admired him *more than anything* for the respect shown him by the Emperor: it felt it saw its own glory in the sacred light—still awesome, but perfectly inoffensive—that shimmered around his brow. The painter of kings could not but be the king of painters: the Queen of the Seas regarded him as her son and, thanks to him, recovered a little majesty. She had, in the past, given him a profession and a reputation, but, when he worked, the radiance of his divine right streamed through the walls and reached as far as the San Marco district. She knew then that he gave back a hundredfold what she had given him: he was a National Treasure.

Furthermore, the man was as long-lived as the trees; he went on for a century and gradually transformed into an institution. The presence of this one-member Academy, born before their time and determined to out-live them, demoralized the young; it exasperated and dis-couraged their ambitions. They felt their city could confer immortality on the living, but that it had reserved that favour for Titian alone. As a victim of this misun-derstanding, Tintoretto demanded the city regard him as the equal of his renowned predecessor, on the falla-cious pretext that he was every bit as worthy. But wor-thiness was not at issue: it is, by right, a question for hereditary monarchies, but not a matter for republics. Jacopo was mistaken when he criticized the City of the Doges for shining all its lights on the baobab of the Rialto. The opposite was the case: that old trunk was illuminated by a beam that had its source in Rome, Madrid or, at any rate, somewhere outside the city's walls; only then did it spill over on to Venice, dragging it from its shadows. It was indirect lighting, so to speak.

I was going to call this chapter 'In the Shadow of Titian', but that was mistaken too, *for Titian cast no shadow*. Just reflect on this: when Jacopo was born, the old man was forty-one years old; when the younger man first attempted to make a name for himself, he was seventy-two. This might be the moment to yield to youth; he could bow out gracefully at that point. But he was having none of it! The indestructible monarch reigned for another twenty-seven years. When he died, aged a hundred, he had the supreme good fortune to leave behind him an unfinished *Pietà*, the way young hopefuls do who are cut down in their prime. For more than half a century, Tintoretto-the-Mole scuttled around in a maze whose walls were bespattered with glory; up to the age of fifty-eight, this creature of the night was hounded by the sunlight radiated by Another, blinded by His implacable celebrity. When that brilliance was finally extinguished, Jacopo Robusti was himself of an age to die. He stubbornly outlived the tyrant, but he was to gain nothing by it: Titian's trick was to combine two contradictory functions and make himself a court painter while retaining the independence of a small master: such a happy conjuncture would not be found often in history. At any rate, we are a long way from it with Tintoretto who put all his eggs in the same basket.

Take a look at the two tombs and you will see what putting his country before all else still costs him, even today. The radioactive corpse of the Old Man was buried under a mountain of lard at Santa Maria dei Frari, effectively the cemetery of the Doges; Tintoretto's body lies beneath a slab in the obscure shade of a local parish church. Personally, I find this entirely appropriate: the lard, sugar and nougat go to Titian: this is poetic justice and I would have been even happier if he had been buried in Rome beneath the monument to Victor Emmanuel, which, with the exception of Milan Central Station, is the most hideous building in the whole of Italy. To Jacopo, the honours of bare stone: his name suffices. But, since this is a strictly personal opinion, I would understand if an indignant traveller were to call on Venice to justify itself: 'Ungrateful city, is this all you could do for the best of your sons?' Why so petty-mindedly surround that Titianesque opera, *The Assumption*, with a bank of lights and yet so meanly begrudge Robusti's canvases electricity? I know what Venice's answer will be: we find it as early as 1549 in Aretino's correspondence: 'If Robusti wishes to be honoured, why does he not paint like Tiziano Vecellio?' Jacopo would hear that refrain every day of his life; it would be repeated before every one of his canvases, before and after his death, and it is still repeated today:

> Where has he gone wrong? Why does he stray from the royal road when he has had the good fortune to find it opened up for him? Our great Vecellio raised painting to such a high degree of perfection that it should never again be changed: either the newcomers will follow in the footsteps of the Master or Art will fall back into barbarism.

Capricious Venetians, illogical bourgeois! Tintoretto is *their* painter; he shows them what they see and feel and they cannot abide him; Titian doesn't give two hoots for them and they adore him. Titian spends the better part of his time reassuring princes, attesting by his paintings that all is for the best in the best of all possible worlds. Discord is merely an illusion; the worst of enemies are secretly reconciled by the colour of their coats. Violence? A ballet danced without much conviction by pseudo-toughs with gentle woolly beards: thus are wars justified. The painter's art verges on apologetics and becomes theodicy: suffering, injustice and evil don't exist. Nor does mortal sin: Adam and Eve transgressed only to gain the opportunity to know—and show us—that they were naked. In a great, four-pronged gesture, at once noble and languid, God leaning down from on high and Man sprawling backwards reach out to one another. Order reigns; perspective, tamed and enslaved, respects the hierarchies: with some discreet adjustments, the best places are reserved for kings and saints. If someone is lost in the distance, in the foggy reaches of a wasteland or the smoky lamplight of some dubious quarter, it is never by chance: the darkness corresponds to the obscurity of his condition and it is, moreover, needed to set off the bright lights of the foreground. The paintbrush pretends to be relating an event, but in fact what it depicts is a ceremony. Sacrificing movement to order and relief to unity, it doesn't so much shape bodies as caress them. Of all the bearded men applauding the Assumption, none has an individual existence. The group appeared first, with its raised arms, its legs—a burning bush; after which this single substance was given a measure of diversity by the production of these transient figures that just stand out from the collective background, but which can, at any moment, be absorbed back into it: this is the condition of the ordinary folk; Titian reserves individuality for the Grandees. Even then he takes care to smooth their corners: relief isolates and distances; it is a form of pessimism. The courtier, a professional optimist, indicates that relief, then mists it over and sets all his colours to sing the glory of God in unison. After which, he sets about polishing his painting: scratching out and buffing up, lacquering and varnishing. He will spare no effort to conceal his labour. In the end he vanishes altogether: you walk into a deserted picture, stroll amid flowers beneath a righteous sun, but the owner is dead; the walker is so alone that he disappears, oblivious. All that remains is that greatest of treacheries: Beauty.

For once the traitor has the excuse that he believes in what he is doing: he isn't a man of the city, but a peasant who has 'made it'; when he came to Venice it was from the countryside and his childhood, from the depths of the Middle Ages. This yokel had for many years felt the people's reverential love of the nobility; he passed through the bourgeoisie without noticing them, joining his true masters in the upper social reaches, all the more certain of pleasing them for the sincerity of his respect. It is often said he regarded himself secretly as their equal: I do not believe this at all. Where would such a conception have come from? He is a vassal: ennobled by the glory only kings can dispense; he owes everything to them, even his pride. Why would he turn this round against them? His impudent happiness, the hierarchy of powers and the beauty of the world are, in his eyes, merely reciprocal reflections; as sincerely as one might ever imagine, he takes the bourgeois techniques of the Renaissance and places them in the service of feudalism: he has stolen the toolkit.

Yet bourgeois and patricians both admire him: he provides Venice's technocrats with an alibi; he speaks of happiness, glory, pre-existent harmony at the very moment when they are making the most praiseworthy efforts to conceal from themselves their decline. All the merchants, whether of lowly or noble birth, are enchanted by these beatific canvases that reflect to them the calm repose of kings. If all is for the best, if evil is merely a fine illusion, if everyone retains forever their hereditary place in the divine and social hierarchy, then none of the events of the last hundred years has happened: the Turks haven't taken Constantinople; Columbus hasn't discovered America; the Portuguese haven't even dreamed of dumping their spices on the world market and the continental powers haven't allied themselves against *la Serenissima*. People had thought that the Barbary pirates were rife on the high seas, that the African source of precious metals had dried up, that the scarcity of money during the first half of the century had put a brake on trade and then, suddenly, that Peruvian gold flowing down in torrents from the great Spanish tank had driven prices up again and swamped the market. But it was merely a dream: Venice still rules over the Mediterranean; it is at the height of its power, wealth and greatness. In other words, these troubled people want Beauty because it is reassuring.

In this, I can understand them. I have flown more than two hundred times now, though I never get used to it. I am too used to crawling about the earth to find flying normal and, from time to time, the fear resurfaces—most particularly when my flying companions are as ugly as I am. But it only takes a beautiful young woman to be on the flight, or a handsome young man, or a charming, loving couple and my fear vanishes. Ugliness is a prophecy: there is in it some unidentifiable extremism that wants to raise negation to the point of horror. The Beautiful seems indestructible; its sacred image protects us: so long as It will remain among us, the catastrophe will not happen. So it was with Venice: the city was beginning to fear it would collapse into the slime of the lagoons; it took the notion of rescuing itself through Beauty, that supreme frivolity; it looked to its palaces and paintings to serve it as life-rafts and rescuing floats. Those who ensured Titian's success were the same people who deserted the sea, who fled disenchantment in orgies, who preferred the security of ground-rents to the profits of commerce.

Tintoretto was born in a distressed city; he breathed the air of Venetian disquiet and it ate away at him; it was all that he knew how to paint. In his place, his severest critics would have acted no differently. But they were not in his place: they could not help but feel this disquiet, but they didn't want to have it shown to them; they condemned the pictures that *represented* it. Jacopo was doomed by ill fate to be the unwitting witness to an age that refused to know itself. This time we discover the meaning of that destiny and the secret of Venetian ill-feeling at a single stroke. Tintoretto displeased everyone: the patricians because he revealed to them the Puritanism and dreamy agitation of the bourgeois; the artisans because he destroyed the corporate order and revealed the seething of hatreds and rivalries beneath the veneer of occupational solidarity; the patriots because, by his hand, the frenzied distraction of painting and the absence of God disclosed an absurd, chance-governed world to them, where anything could happen—*even* the death of Venice. But surely this newly bourgeois painter was at least palatable to his adoptive class. Unfortunately not: the bourgeoisie didn't accept him unreservedly: he constantly fascinated them, but often he scared them. This was because they were a class that was not yet self-aware. Master Zignioni doubtless dreamed of betrayal; he was obscurely seeking the means of joining the patricians, in short, of leaving behind that bourgeois reality which he contributed, despite himself, to producing: what he loathed most in Robusti's paintings was their radicalism and their demystifying power. In short, Tintoretto's testimony had at all costs to be rejected, his efforts presented as a failure and the originality of his experimentation denied: *he had to be got rid of.*

When we look at what he was criticized for, it was *first and foremost*, for working too quickly and leaving the mark of his hand everywhere; it was polished, finished work that was wanted—above all something *impersonal.* If the painter revealed himself in the work, he put himself at issue; and if he put himself at issue, he posed a challenge to the public. Venice imposed the Puritans' maxim on its painters—'no personal remarks': it would make every effort to confound Jacopo's lyricism with the haste of an overworked supplier who performs slapdash work. Then there is the following piece of tittle-tattle reported by Ridolfi: Tintoretto is said to have written up on the walls of his studio: 'Titian's colour and Michelangelo's representation of relief.' This is stupid: that formula is found only at a very late date, being coined by a Venetian art critic with no reference whatever to Robusti. In fact, Tintoretto could have known Michelangelo's works only through Daniele de Volterra's reproductions—hence in 1557 *at the earliest.* And who do they take him for? Do they think he would *seriously* devote himself to concocting such an absurd potion? It is, in fact, a fantasy of the period: in the face of the Spanish threat, the cities of northern and middle Italy sought to unite, but did so too late. Yet the awakening of a national consciousness—rapidly put to sleep again—was not without its transient influence on the Fine Arts. 'Michelangelo and Titian' means Florence and Venice. How fine that would be: painting unified!

There is nothing serious in this, as we can see: the dream is a harmless one so long as it remains everybody's. But those who claim to see it as the obsession of Robusti *alone* must have wanted to tear that artist in two by lodging an explosive nightmare in his breast. Colour is *Jean-qui-rit*, the representation of relief is *Jean-qui-pleure*. On the one hand, unity; on the other, a permanent risk of disorder. On the one side, the harmony of the spheres; on the other, abandonment. The century's two Titans hurl themselves at each other, grab each other by the throat and attempt strangulation: Jacopo is the theatre of operations. At times Titian wins a round, but only just; at others Michelangelo is the victor, but with difficulty. In any event, the loser has enough strength left to spoil the victor's triumph: the result of the Pyrrhic victory is a failed painting. Failed from excess: Tintoretto seems to contemporaries like a Titian gone mad, devoured by the dark passion of Buonarroti, shaking with Saint Vitus' Dance—a case of possession, a curious dual personality. In a sense, Jacopo does not exist, except as a battlefield; in another sense, he is a monster, a misbegotten creature. Vasari's story now has a strange light cast upon it: Adam Robusti wanted to taste the fruit of the tree of knowledge and the Archangel Tiziano, with outstretched finger and beating wings, drove him out of Paradise.

Even today, to be the victim or the bringer of bad luck is one and the same thing in Italy. If you have recently had financial difficulties, a car accident or a broken leg, or if your wife has just left you, don't expect to be invited to dinner: a hostess will not lightly expose her other guests to premature baldness, a head cold or, in extreme cases, to the risk of breaking their necks on her stairs. I know a Milanese who has the evil eye; it was discovered last year: he no longer has any friends and dines at home alone. Jacopo is like this: a caster of fate, because his fate has been cast—or his mother's, perhaps, when she was carrying him. In fact, the *jettatura* comes from Venice: the city, accursed and worried, produced a worried man; it curses its own worrying nature in him. The unfortunate man is desperately in love with a city that is in despair but will not admit it: the love-object is horrified by such love. When Tintoretto passes, people draw aside: he reeks of death. This is perfectly true. But what do the patrician festivals, the bourgeois charity and the docility of the people smell of, if not the very same thing? Or the redbrick houses with their flooded cellars and their walls striped with horizontal rat-runs? What do these stagnant canals smell of, with their urinal-style watercress and these grey mussels locked in their foul, gooey coating beneath the quays? At the bottom of a *rio*, there is a bubble stuck to the clay; it is shaken clear by the backwash from the gondolas and rises through the muddy water, emerges on the surface, revolves, glistens, bursts with a silent fart and everything dies with it: bourgeois nostalgias, the grandeur of the Republic, God and Italian painting.

Tintoretto led the mourning for Venice and for a world. But when he died, no one lamented his passing and then silence descended. Hypocritically pious hands covered his canvases in veils of mourning. If we tear down this black veil, we shall find a portrait started over again a hundred times. The portrait of Jacopo? Of the Queen of the Seas? As you like: the city and its painter have but a single face.

Les Temps Modernes, 141
(November 1957).

A FINE DISPLAY OF CAPUCHINS[1]

Three o'clock: the storm catches me on the Nomentana in the north-west of the city. It is a raging of birds: a whirl of plumage, a screeching, black feathers flying up to the sky. When calm has returned, I feel my jacket. It is dry. A straw sun is already breaking through the grey-blue cotton wool of the clouds. To the west, broad and empty, a street climbs between the houses and ends in the sky. I can never resist the temptation to ascend these little hills to see what's on the other side. The finest in Europe is rue Rochechouart, when viewed from Boulevard Barbès. Once you've crested the pass, you almost expect to glimpse the sea. The rain is coming down again and bouts of spray hit me as I climb. A smear of bitumen sprawls down from the top of the hill and settles against the sickly pallor of a wall. That wall puts an end to Rome's imposture: beyond it, there is a cabbage patch,

---

1 The French title of this piece, 'Un parterre de Capucines', plays on the word *capucine*, which means both a Capuchin nun and a nasturtium. [Trans.]

an expanse of acid light, the last vestige of humanity; and then wilderness. A wilderness in the rain. Far away, the blue-black ink of the Alban Hills fades into the sky. This land-locked city is more alone in the environing lands than a boat on the sea.

Taxi to the Via Vittorio Veneto, autumnal and bourgeois. The street of the rich foreigners. But the rich foreigners are hiding in their hotels. On the pavements and on the steps of Santa Maria della Concezione, the plane trees, shaken by the storm, have shed their leaves, which are the colour of Roman walls. You might think the *palazzi* were moulting. Ochre, bright red, chrome yellow in the puddles: a marinade of dead skins. Santa Maria della Concezione is the Capuchin church. I go in. The nave is deserted. Silence, nothing. St Michael is noiselessly crushing the Devil's head; gilded chandeliers ring the altar. At the far end, on the right, near the sacristy, forestalling my questions, a sullen friar puts his left index finger to his lips and points me to a stairway plunging underground. His left hand, suspended for a moment in the air, is rounded, cupped and pressed against my stomach. I give him twenty lire and pass along. I go down some stairs and find myself in a gallery of catacombs: the crypt. But no: the left-hand wall has some barred windows in it; stretching up, I can see a little garden through the bars: I am in a hospital corridor. There is a thoroughly Italian ambiguity in this: I am on the ground floor in the cold, clear light of autumn and in the basement in the yellow glow of electric light bulbs. On the right, the corridor runs past four small rooms of unequal size: mortuary chapels, little cells protected by low balustrades that remind me both of communion rails and of the ropes that cordon off the drawing-rooms in stately homes. For that reason, as I come closer, the chapels become drawing-rooms. Four little rococo boudoirs, whose walls, white beneath the grime, are flanked by dark niches, alcoves or divan-beds in their lower part and, in the upper section, decorated with pleasing, artless arabesques, with rosettes, ellipses and stars, all quite crudely executed. The only odd thing about the decoration and the furnishings is the material they are made of: it is bone. What ingenuity! To make a cherub takes just a skull and two shoulder-blades; the shoulder-blades will be the wings. By tastefully piling up skulls and femurs, you get rock-work niches. The old chandeliers themselves, providing an illumination that pales in the daylight, are bundles of tibias hanging from the ceiling by chains. Each *salotto* has its own inhabitants: standing by its bed, a skeleton in a homespun robe salutes me; a mummy sits up on its couch. You might think these corpses were for sale: there are tickets on their robes, but no prices marked, just their names and social rank. Here is the Grim Reaper above my head, floating, with his hourglass and scythe: I'm not sure whether he's swimming or flying, but the air around him coagulates into a troubling gelatinous mass. Between the three walls of each *salotto*, beneath a blackish compost, its grains shining and tightly packed—anthracite dust or caviar?—

a number of more privileged monks are taking their rest. This humus is the soil known as consecrated ground: an inscription on a cross planted bang in the middle of the sacred plot tells us as much, like the tags indicating plant names in a botanical garden. *Terra Sancta*: a species of tufa not native to these parts: it is found principally in Palestine, with other varieties in Lhasa, Mecca and elsewhere. I gaze at the baroque incrustations on the walls and wonder why the Capuchins have broken the nitrogen cycle and preserved these organic products from dissolution. Did they wish to show that everything sings the glory of God, even those peculiar pipes we are made of? I should like to think so. But why these exceptions? Why perch that skeleton on this pile of sticks that once were men? Why provide this carefully reconstructed prior with such a bed of bones? The living have used other dead bodies to serve those that are themselves mere dust and grimaces. It reminds me of a postcard I used to look at in the window of a newsagent's on the Boulevard Saint-Michel when I was a child: from a distance you could see the head of the Little Corporal, Napoleon Bonaparte. Closer up, the head began to swarm; it became a tangle of maggots. Nearer still, and the maggots were nudes. The delight in humiliating great men— the eye of the victor of Austerlitz was nothing but a buttock—combined with the delights of humiliating women: the most beautiful woman in the world, pressed up against a great many others, is worthy only to serve as conjunctive tissue for the male. It is not God we find in these chapels, but the image of a circle of hell: the exploitation of one dead man by another. Bones circle around other bones, all alike, making up that other rose-like figure: a skeleton. I am startled by someone speaking next to me. 'Good heavens! To think you can make human beings out of thigh bones, shins and skulls.' A fat Italian with fierce eyes falls to one knee, crosses himself, springs nimbly to his feet and scurries away. Two French women are torn between admiration and terror.

'My sister-in-law found it upsetting, but I don't. Does it upset you?'

'No, it doesn't.'

'No, me neither. It's so . . .'

'So well-ordered. So well-presented.'

Well-presented is right. And above all, it's made from nothing. I imagine Picasso would be delighted. 'A box of matches!' he said once. 'A box of matches that would be a box of matches and, *at the same time,* a frog!' He would like these elbow-bones that are both elbow-bones and the spokes of a wheel. In fact, the material counts more in this masterpiece than the form. It is a sorry material, but sufficient to horrify. It is not really brittle or friable; and yet how fragile it is: it has that dull life you find in hair that keeps on growing after death. If I tried to break it, it would crack lengthways against my palm, a bundle of splinters that would bend without breaking. Faced with this dubious joinery, dead and alive, rough and smooth, I draw back and slip my hands into my pockets: touch nothing, brush against nothing. I have sealed up my mouth hermetically, but there are always the damned nostrils: in all such dubious places, they dilate and the surroundings come streaming in in the form of a smell. There's a hint of a smell of bones. It's a mixture: one quarter old plaster, three quarters bug infestation. And for all that I tell myself I am imagining it, there's nothing to be done: I have four thousand Capuchins up my nose. Because there were four thousand of them that had to be dug up one by one. I would locate somewhere around 1810 the germinal frenzy that triggered this sadistic lyricism among honest monks and drove them to dash around on all fours sniffing the ground to unearth these sizeable truffles. It seems other examples are to be found. There is one at Palermo, I'm told. Towards the end of the French occupation, the order of Capuchins must have caught a heavy dose of pre-Romanticism.

'They've no right to do this!'

Upset and angry, a very beautiful woman stops on the bottom step and turns towards her ageing husband coming down behind her.

'They've no right!'

She has spoken too loudly: the Frenchwomen are staring at her. Embarrassed, her husband smiles apologetically.

'Well, they were monks . . .'

She raises here lovely, rancorous eyes to the cherubs:

'It's not permissible,' she says emphatically.

I smile at her; she is right: it is not permissible. But who or what is to forbid it? Christianity, perhaps, but not the Church, which makes a profit from this *capucinade.*[2] Yet surely it isn't Christian to play jigsaws with an ossuary. Desecration of graves, sadism, necrophilia—this is all blatant sacrilege. My compatriots cross themselves: these ladies are under a misapprehension: they have come to pay their respects to death in a place where death is scoffed at. I forgive them: beneath their dresses, they may perhaps have stockings worn threadbare at the knees on the steps of the Scala Santa; perhaps, this very morning, they saw the telegrams piling up at Santa Maria di Aracoeli around a doll swaddled in gold cloth; you need to be hard-headed in Rome to distinguish religion from witchcraft. If these good mothers had not, without realizing it, been changed into witches, they would not confuse the thrill they feel with the pious disgust preachers inspire when they describe the decay of the flesh. The lofty condemnation of the body we find in some Spanish paintings—that is good Catholicism. Shall we show kings eaten by worms? Well and good! The maggots make a shimmering silky surplice for their torn purple robes; clumps of macaroni are coming out of their eye sockets and despite that—because of that—

---

2 Though the term is used more freely here, it generally means a dull sermon or address. [Trans.]

these bodies remain ghastly images of ourselves: they are men decomposing; death is a human adventure. In short, it is permissible to mock a corpse, but only down to the bones. The flesh flows aside and frees the three-penny-bits that were concealed in the pudding; after that, with your soul in heaven and your mineral remains on earth, you have earned your rest. Look, rather, at the calm face of death, the tidy decease to which the feminine bones of the Protestant cemetery attest: those old maids are pure mineral. But here, the Capuchin canker attacks the bones. What heresy! To show such zeal over these rotten scraps, you would have to believe they still have a soul in them. And what hatred! These Capuchins are the ancestors of the Milanese crowd that slapped the face of Mussolini when he was dead and hanging by his feet. For hatred, death is a scandal: deprived of its prey, it is left dumbfounded before the detested corpse, like a man who has just been cured of his hiccups. These monks preserve human remains in order to extend the pleasure, they refuse to let human beings become non-descript, in order to be able to treat them like things; they wrest bones from their mineral fate so as to enslave them to the caricature of a human order; they exhume them with great pomp to turn them into building materials. Monks used to consider beauty diabolical when it was merely worldly, but when it is a question of preferring everything, even beauty, to their neighbour, they turn into aesthetes. They deck their chapels out with human relics the way the guards at Buchenwald made lampshades from human skin. Approaching a notice, I find the words: 'No writing on the skulls.' Really? Why not? Armchairs, couches, rock-work, chandeliers, altars . . . why shouldn't these bones also be used as paper, paperweights or blotting paper? It would complete the degradation if one of these bald heads bore the inscription: 'Pierre and Maryse made love here.' But no: the Capuchins' best trick is to have forced the living to adore their victims. The two ladies have left, the beautiful Italian woman is going off down the corridor with a handkerchief pressed to her nose; and I am going too, leaving behind this debris of bones bewitched by a hatred stronger than death. The Capuchin friar is still there, sullen and bearded, by the sacristy. I pass by without glancing in his direction, a little embarrassed, like a client passing the brothel-keeper's assistant: he knows what I have just been seeing; my skeleton walks past his. I go outside. It's raining. All cities are the same in the rain. Paris is no longer in Paris, or London in London; but Rome remains in Rome. A black sky has settled over the houses, the air has changed to water and it is difficult now to make out shapes. But thirty centuries have impregnated the walls with a sort of phosphorus: I walk along in the rain between soft shafts of solar light. The Romans are running among these drowned suns, laughing and waving some ancient implements they don't quite seem to know how to use: umbrellas. I emerge into an underwater square amid drowned carcases. The rain stops, the earth emerges: the carcases are ruins: a temple, an obelisk—in a word, skeletons. I walk round the pillaged Pantheon; the metal-tipped obelisk is supported by an elephant that doesn't look at all happy. This whole African ensemble is there to the glory of Christianity. And here is Rome, emerging from the water, already dry: the whole thing an accursed ossuary. The Church rounded on the monuments of Antiquity the way the Capuchin friars rounded on their colleagues; when the Popes stole the bronze of the Pantheon to ensure Christ's triumph over the pagans, it was the same desecration of graves. Antiquity *is alive* in Rome, with a hate-filled, magical life, because it has been prevented from dying entirely so that it can be kept in bondage. From this it has gained this insidious eternity and has been able to enslave us in its turn: if we are tempted to sacrifice ourselves to these stones, it is because they are bewitched; the order of the ruins fascinates us because it is both human and inhuman: human because it was established by men, inhuman because it stands alone, pickled in the alcohol of Christian hatred, and because it is self-contained, sinister, gratuitous, like the display of Capuchins I have just left.

France-Observateur, 115
(24 July 1952).

*

VENICE FROM MY WINDOW

The water is too well-behaved: you don't hear it. Growing suspicious, I lean out: the sky has fallen in there. The water hardly dares move and its millions of creases confusedly rock the sullen Relic, which blazes up intermittently. Over towards the East, the canal comes to a stop and the vast milky pool begins that reaches as far as Chioggia. But on that side, it is the water that has taken the day off: my gaze skids over a glazed surface, slides over it and peters out towards the Lido, in a dismal incandescence. It is cold; a nondescript day is ushered in in chalky tones; Venice thinks it is Amsterdam once again; those grey pallors in the distance are palaces.

That's how it is here: air, water, fire and stone are continually mingling or changing places, exchanging their natures or their natural locations, playing 'puss in the corner' or 'off-ground tag': old-fashioned games, with nothing innocent about them; we are seeing the training of an illusionist. To inexpert tourists, this unstable compound holds many surprises: while you are putting your nose in the air to see what the weather will be like, the whole of the heavens with its clouds and atmospheric phenomena may well be lying at your feet distilled into a silvery ribbon. For example, it may very well be that an early morning Assumption has spirited the lagoon away today and placed it where the sky ought to be. I look up: no, there is nothing there but a vertiginous hole, with neither light nor shade, rent solely by the colourless beams of cosmic rays. On the surface of this upturned abyss, a pointlessly frothing foam conceals the undoubted absence of the Sun. As soon as it can, that celestial body slips away; it is fully aware that it is undesirable and that Venice persists in regarding it as the hated image of personal rule. In fact, the city consumes more light than Palermo or Tunis, especially if you count the amount absorbed by the high-walled, dark alleyways; but Venice will not have it said that she owes her illumination to the liberality of a single source.

We must here consult the legend: in the beginning, the lagoon was plunged into perpetual radiant night; the patricians liked to view the constellations, whose equilibrium, based on mutual mistrust, reminded them of the benefits of aristocratic rule. All was for the best: the Doges, kept under close surveillance, were resigned to being no more than the straw men of commercial capitalism. One of them, Faliero, cuckolded and publicly mocked, rebelled against this briefly, but was immediately thrown into jail. His judges had no difficulty persuading him of his guilt: he had incurred the death penalty by attempting to impede the forward march of the historical Process, but, if he acknowledged his guilt, posterity would honour his misplaced courage. So he did, indeed, die craving the people's forgiveness and praising the justice that was to be done to him. Since then, no one had disturbed public order; Venice was peaceful beneath her seven stars.

The Grand Council decided to decorate its Council Chamber by having the high frieze painted with the portraits of past Doges, and, when they came to Faliero, these vindictive merchants ordered that his picture be covered with a veil bearing the insulting words: *Hic est locus Marini Falieri decapitati pro criminibus*. Now the poor lamb really lost his temper: was this what he had been promised? Not only was posterity not rehabilitating him but his memory was forever to be execrated. Suddenly, his severed head rose on the horizon and began to revolve above the city; the sky and the lagoon became tinged with purple and the proud patricians on the Piazza San Marco hid their eyes behind horrified fingers and cried out: '*Ecco Marino*'. Since then, he has returned every twelve hours, the city has been haunted and, as ancient custom demands that the Doge-elect appear on his balcony to throw jewels and florins to the crowd, the murdered Potentate ironically casts waves of gold sullied with his blood across the squares.

This myth has today been shown to be without foundation; beneath the vestibule of the chapel of the Madonna della Pace, in SS Giovanni e Paulo, a sarcophagus was discovered containing a human skeleton with its head on its knees. So, everything returned to normal, except that the Venetians, unyielding in their resentment, immediately converted the sarcophagus into a water-trough. No matter; we can judge the people's state of mind and their animosity against the day star by this story, which the gondoliers willingly relate. The city certainly likes to see the treasure it has won on the seas reflected in the golden sky, but only provided that it remains skewered up above it like the straggling mark of its greatness, or summer embroiders it in emblematic flashes across the heavy green draperies that stretch, by its good offices, down into the Canal. In Rome, that great inland village, I am, in fact, always happy to be present at the birth of an earthbound king. But when I have spent some time drifting around the canals of Venice, and seen copper-coloured fumes rising above the Rio or ephemeral glimmering lights take flight above my head, I can only admire this system of indirect lighting and it is not without a sense of unease that I step out again on to the Riva degli Schiavoni and see the great, worn face of Marino Faliero floating above the subtle shimmerings of the town.

No sun today, then. It is playing at being Louis XVI in Paris or Charles I in London. By disappearing, the great golden orb has disturbed the equilibrium; what remains are shafts of light, with no top or bottom to them; the landscape revolves, and I revolve with it, now hanging by my feet above an absence, beneath the frescoes of the Canal, now standing on a promontory above a shipwrecked sky. We revolve, the ceiling, the floor and I, who am the Ixion on this wheel, in the most absolute immobility. I end up feeling seasick: the emptiness is unbearable. But there you are: in Venice, nothing is simple. Because it is not a city, but an archipelago. How could you forget that? From your little island you look enviously across at the one opposite. What is there over there? A solitude, a purity and a silence which, you could swear, are not to be found over here. Wherever you are, you always find the real Venice is elsewhere. At least, it's like that for me. Normally, I'm reasonably happy with my lot, but, in Venice, I fall prey to a sort of jealous madness. If I didn't restrain myself, I'd be constantly on the bridges or in gondolas, madly seeking out the secret Venice on the other bank. Needless to say, as soon as I reach that bank, everything withers. I turn around and the mysterious peace has now descended on the other side. I have long been resigned to this: Venice is wherever I am not.

Those princely houses opposite are *rising out of* the water, are they not? It's impossible for them to be floating—houses don't float—or for them to be resting on the lagoon: it would sink under their weight. Or for them to be weightless: you can see they are built of brick, stone and wood. What, then? You cannot but *feel* them emerging. To look the palaces on the Grand Canal up and down is to discover that they are caught in a sort of frozen upthrust, which is, if you like, the reversal of their density, the inversion of their mass. A surge of petrified water: you would think they had just appeared and nothing had been there before these stubborn little erections. In short, they always have something of the *apparition* about them. With an apparition, you guess what it might be. It might be said to come into being instantaneously, the better to hammer home the paradox: pure nothingness still persists, but this entity is already there too. When I look at the Palazzo Dario, leaning to one side, seeming to leap out aslant, I always feel that it is—very much—there, but, at the same time, nothing is. All the more so as it sometimes happens that the whole city vanishes. One evening, when I was coming back from Murano, my boat was alone for as far as the eye could see. There was no Venice any longer. Where the disaster had occurred, the water was covered in dust beneath the gold of the sky. For the moment, everything was clear and precise. All those fine plumes of silence were present and correct, but they don't *satisfy you* the way a great rugged mountain landscape does, tumbling down beneath your windows, in utter abandon. Are they waiting or defiant? These pretty things have a provocative reserve about them. And then, what is there facing me here? The *Other* pavement of a 'residential' avenue or the *Other* bank of a river? In any event, *it is the Other*. If truth be told, the left and right

of the Canal are not so dissimilar. The Fondaco dei
Turchi is, of course, on one side and the Ca' d'Oro on
the other. But, broadly speaking, you have the same little
boxes, the same marquetry work, interrupted here and
there by the roar of those great white marble city halls,
eaten away by tears of dirt. At times, as my gondola slid
down between these two funfairs, I wondered which was
the reflection of the other. In short, it isn't their differ-
ences that separate them: quite the opposite. Imagine
you were to go up to a mirror; an image forms in it: your
nose, your eyes, your mouth, your suit. It is you, it
should be you. And yet there's something in the reflection—something that is neither the green of your eyes,
nor the shape of your lips, nor the cut of your suit—
that makes you suddenly say they have put *someone else*
in the mirror, in place of my reflection. This is roughly
the impression the 'Venices opposite' make at any time
of day. Nothing would stop me believing today that *our*
funfair is the real one and the other merely its image,
blown off slightly to the East by the Adriatic wind. Just
now, as I opened my window, I made a similar window
open on the third floor of the Palazzo Loredan, which
is this building's double. Logically, I should even have
appeared in it, but it was, instead, a woman who poked
her head out, leaned over towards the water, unfurled a
carpet like a roll of parchment and began to beat it
abstractedly. And this matutinal beating, the only movement to be seen, soon abated; it was swallowed up by
the darkness of the room and the window closed upon

it. Forsaken, the miniatures are carried off in a motionless glide. But this isn't what troubles me: together, we are drifting. There is something else, a very slight, systematic strangeness, which vanishes whenever I attempt to pin it down, but returns as soon as I start to think of something else. When I look out of my window in Paris, I often find it impossible to understand the merry-go-round of sparkling little people gesticulating on the terrace of the *Deux Magots* and I never knew why, one Sunday, they leapt out of their seats and ran over to a Cadillac parked by the pavement and jostled it, laughing. No matter: what they do, I do with them; from my lookout post, I too shook the Cadillac, because they are my natural crowd. I need only a minute, at the very most, to be down there with them; and when I lean out to look at them, I am already among them, looking up at my window, with their crazy ideas running through my head. I can't even say precisely that I *look* at them, since, when it comes down to it, I have never seen them. I *touch* them. Why? Because there is a terrestrial path between us, the Earth's reassuring crust. The *Others* are beyond the seas.

The *other* Venice is beyond the sea. Two women in black come down the steps of Santa Maria della Salute. They scuttle across the square, accompanied by their pale shadows, and on to the bridge that leads to San Gregorio. They are suspect and marvellous. They are women, but women as distant as those Arabs I saw from

Spain, bowing down upon the soil of Africa. *Weird and wonderful*: they are the inhabitants of these untouchable houses, the Holy Women from Beyond the Seas. And here is another untouchable, the man who has planted himself in front of the church they have just left and who is looking at it, as is no doubt their wont on this unknown island. He is, horror of horrors, *mon semblable, mon frère*; he has a *Blue Guide* in his left hand and a Rolleiflex slung over his shoulder. Who could be more bereft of mystery than a tourist? Well, this one, frozen in his dubious stillness, is as troubling as the savages in horror films who part the rushes, watch the heroine go by with a glint in their eye and then disappear. He is a tourist from the Other Venice and I shall never see what he sees. Opposite me, these brick and marble walls have the fleeting strangeness of those solitary hillside villages you see from a train window.

All this is on account of the Canal. Were it just an honest stretch of sea, candidly admitting that its function was to keep human beings apart, or a raging river that had been tamed, carrying its little craft along reluctantly, there would be nothing to make a fuss about: we would just say there's a certain city over there, different from our own and, by that very token, entirely like it. A city like any other. But this Canal claims to *bring people together*; it presents itself as a watery path, deliberately made for walking on. The stone steps that run down to the roadway, like the white front steps of the pink villas in Baltimore, the carriage entrances that should open to let out a pony and trap, the little brick walls protecting the garden from the curiosity of passers-by and the long tresses of honeysuckle running along the walls and trailing down to the ground—all this is prompting me to run across the carriageway and establish that the tourist on the far side really is one of my own kind and that he isn't seeing anything I can't. But the temptation vanishes before it has altogether taken shape; it has no effect other than to heighten my imagination: I can already feel the ground opening up; the Canal is just an old branch, rotting away beneath its moss, beneath the dry black hulls covering it, which crack if you set foot on them. I am going under, I am sinking, with my arms upraised, and the last thing I see will be the indecipherable face of the Unknown Man on the Far Bank, who has now turned round to look at me, anxiously gauging his impotence in the situation or enjoying the sight of me falling into the trap. In short, this false connection only pretends to bring things together, the better to keep them apart; it thwarts my plans with ease and gives me to believe that communication with my fellow men is impossible; even the tourist's proximity is an optical illusion, like the striped creatures that the 'Newly Weds of the Eiffel Tower' mistook for bees when they were actually desert tigers.[1] Venice's water lends the whole city a mildly nightmarish coloration: it is in nightmares that tools let

---

1 *Les Mariés de la Tour Eiffel* (1921) is a one-act ballet written to a scenario by Jean Cocteau. [Trans.]

us down, that the revolver levelled at the mad killer
doesn't go off; it is in nightmares that we are running
with a deadly enemy at our heels when suddenly the
road starts to melt as we try to cross it.

The tourist, still shrouded in mystery, leaves the
scene. He goes on to the little bridge and disappears. I
am alone above the motionless Canal. The far bank
seems even more inaccessible today. The sky has rent the
water, which is in tatters; who would believe the Canal
had a bottom to it? Through the great grey lagoons with
which it is studded, I see the sky shining beneath the
water. Between the two quays there is *nothing*: a transparent sash hastily thrown across a void. Those cottages
are separated from ours by a crevice running across the
whole of the earth. Two halves of Europe are separating.
They move apart gently at first, then faster and faster;
as in *Hector Servadac*,[2] now is the time to wave hand-
kerchiefs. But the far quay is deserted, all the windows
are closed. Already there are *two* human races, their des-
tinies already dividing for all time, but no one knows it
yet. In an hour's time, a maid will step out on to some
balcony to beat the carpets and be aghast at the void
beneath her and a great yellow and grey mass revolving
ten thousand leagues away. Venice is constantly breaking
up; whether I'm on the Riva degli Schiavoni, looking

---

2 Jules Verne, *Hector Servadac, voyages et aventures à travers le monde
solaire* (Paris: Pierre-Jules Hetzel, 1877); *Hector Servadac; Or the
Career of a Comet* (Ellen Frewer trans.) (New York: Scribner Arm-
strong, 1878). [Trans.]

towards San Giorgio, or on the Nuova Fondamenta looking towards Burano, I always have a Land's End opposite me, emerging from a chaotic sterility, from some vain interstellar agitation. This morning, the precious architecture opposite, which I never took entirely seriously before, seems fearfully austere: these are the smooth walls of a human world moving away; a little world, so limited, so enclosed, rising up definitively like a thought in the middle of a desert. *I am not in it.* The floating island is the whole earth, round and overloaded with human beings; it is moving away and I am left on the quayside. In Venice and a few other places, you have the time to view the destiny of man from outside, with the eyes of an angel or an ape. Sadly, we weren't there for Noah's Ark. Of course, last summer, off the North Cape, we had this impression even more strongly: it seemed a fact or almost. We were bouncing around; to the south the last claws of Europe scratched at the sea, to our north were millions of grey waves, the solitude of a dead star. I ended up thinking I was in interstellar space, a satellite revolving around an inaccessible Earth. You don't feel the same anxiety in Venice and yet Humanity moves away from you, sliding off over a calm lake. The human race—or, who knows, the historical Process—retracts, to become a little seething ferment, limited in space and time. I see it whole, from some point outside time and space, and very gently, very treacherously, sense my abandonment.

The present is what I touch; it is the tool I can handle; it is what is acting on me or what I can change. These pretty chimeras are not my present. Between them and me there is no simultaneity. All it takes is a little sun to turn them into promises; perhaps they are coming to me from the depths of the future. On some spring mornings, I have seen them advancing towards me, a floating garden, still *other*, but like a portent, a presage of what I shall be tomorrow. But the sullen brightness of this morning has killed their colours and walled them up in their finitude. They are flat and inert; the general drift of things carries them away from me. They are definitely not part of my experience; they well up from the distant depths of a memory that is in the process of forgetting them—a strange, anonymous memory, the memory of sky and water. In Venice, the tiniest thing is enough to turn light into a gaze. A certain light has only to envelop this imperceptible insular distance, this constant gap between things, for that light to seem like a thought; it kindles or erases the meanings scattered about the floating clusters of houses. This morning I read Venice in the eyes of another; a glassy stare has settled on the false grove, wilting the sugar candy roses and the lilies made of bread dipped in milk; everything is in a glass case; I am present at the awakening of a gloomy memory. From the depths of an ancient gaze my eyes try to dredge up sunken palaces, but retrieve only generalities. Am I perceiving or remembering? I see what I know. Or, rather, what another already knows. *Another* memory is haunting mine, Another's recollections well up before me, a frozen flight of dead parakeets; everything has a weary air of the past, of having been seen before. The San Gregorio Abbey garden is just greenery, the simplified rose windows mere working drawings; the facades, those sad, severe colourwashes beyond a glacial lake, offer themselves with perfect clarity—almost too perfect, crystalline—but I cannot pin down any detail. Little houses, little palaces, fine follies, bankers' and ship-owners' whims, the Capriccio Loredano, the Barbaro folly—you are all virtually digested, almost half-way dissolved into generalities. The Gothic Idea is applied to the Moorish Idea; the Idea of marble joins with the Idea of pink; the garnet-coloured blinds and the rotting wood shutters are merely now a water-colourist's brush-strokes: a little green, a patch of burnt topaz. What will remain in this memory, as little by little it forgets? A long red and white wall, then nothing. The palaces, even now being forgotten, are beyond waiting for: they are no longer on the far side of the water, but in a very recent past, yesterday perhaps, or a moment ago; without mov-ing they grow distant, they have lost the naïve brutality of presence, that silly, peremptory smugness of a thing that is there *and cannot be denied*. All that it is possible to love when we love something: chance features, scars, gashes, the poisonous softness of moss, water and old age—is condensed, nay erased, by this urgent, superficial light; there is no space in these things now, but a kind of extension without parts: they are things known, their

matter is worn to the point of transparency, and the joy-
ous coarseness of being attenuates to the point of
absence. They are not there. Not entirely there. I see
their architects' plans and drawings. The dull, false gaze
of death has frozen these winsome sirens, fixing them in
a supreme contortion. Wherever I go today, I am sure
to arrive five minutes too late and to meet only with the
impersonal memory of the disaster, sky and water merg-
ing again, recalling for a moment a drowned city, before
breaking up and scattering into a pure spray of space.
How superfluous I am going to feel, as the only presence
amidst universal obsolescence, and at great risk of
exploding, like one of those deep-sea fish when they are
brought to the surface, because we are used to living
under infinite pressure and such rarefactions are no good
to us. There are days like this here: Venice is content
merely to remember itself and the tourist wanders in
bewilderment through this *cabinet fantastique* in which
water is the central illusion.

A hope: a false ray of sunshine, born of an absence
somewhere, a mere refraction of the void, lights up the
copper figure of *Fortuna* on the Customs House globe,
lathers up the soapy whitenesses of Santa Maria, repaints
naïve and minutely tufted foliage through the abbey's
iron railings, changes the idea of green into wooden
shutters and the idea of topaz into old blinds eaten into
by salt and sky. It passes a languid finger over the dried-
out facades and brings the entire clump of roses into
bloom. This whole suspended little world awakens. At

the same time, a heavy black hull appears in the west: a barge. In its excitement, the water comes alive beneath its burden of sky, shakes its white plumage and turns over; the sky, disturbed, cracks and, pulverized, studs the waves with gleaming maggots. The barge turns and disappears into the shadow of a rio; it was a false alarm; the water reluctantly calms itself and gathers its disorder into heavy, trembling masses; already large patches of azure are re-emerging . . . A sudden release of pigeons: the sky, crazed with fear, is taking flight, the landing-stage beneath my window creaks and attempts to mount the wall: the *vaporetto* goes by, its passage announced by the lowing of a conch. This long, beige cigar is a throwback to Jules Verne and the Exhibition of 1875. There is no one on deck, but its wide wooden benches are still haunted by the bearded gentlemen of the *Cronstadt* who opened the Exhibition. On a little beige-coloured zinc roof over the rear deck, wreaths are lying in piles of three: perhaps they are thrown into the water as floating monuments to commemorate drownings. On the bow, a winged victory in a fur coat abandons herself to the winds. Around her blonde hair, she has knotted a muslin shawl which flaps against her neck: a dreamy passenger from 1900. There is no one to be seen, except this dead woman who knew Wagner and Verdi. A miniature ghost ship is carrying an Italian countess, who died in the wreck of the Titanic, between two ancient celebrations. This is not surprising: each morning the Grand Canal

is covered with anachronisms. It is a floating museum:
the managements parade collectors' items in front of the
loggias of the great hotels—the Gritti, the Luna, the
Bauer-Grunewald. The water laughs gleefully, it plays:
beneath the boat's stem, there's a general stampede;
moorhens jostle, flap away clucking, their panic coming
to rest at my feet. Gondolas and other boats caper
around the great, barbarous gilded posts, their stripes
like those of American barbers' poles. The *vaporetto* is
far in the distance by now, but I am witness to a whole
nautical cavalcade—spume, water nymphs, sea horses.
On the quay, the ray of sunshine has vanished, plunging
the buildings back into generality. The silence proudly
rises in red bricks above this impotent chatter. A distant
trumpet sounds and falls silent. This is a picture for the
tourists: eternity ringed by becoming or the intelligible
World floating above matter. There is still some squawk-
ing beneath my windows, but never mind: silence has
cut down the noises with its icy scythe. In Venice, silence
is visible; it is the taciturn defiance of the Other Bank.
Suddenly, the entire sea-borne parade sinks; the water is
like a dream, with no continuity to its ideas: it is suddenly smooth again and I am leaning out over a great
clump of torpor; it is as though it envied the corpse-like
rigidity of the palaces on its banks. The defiant sky has
not re-descended from the celestial vault; the fake corpse
is turning green between the quays and I can already see
the pale reflection of the Palazzo Dario emerging on the

right. I look up: everything is as it was. I need massive, weighty presences; I feel empty when faced with these fine feathers painted on glass. I'm going out.

Verve, 27–28 (February 1953).

✳

A NOTE ON SOURCES

'The Captive of Venice'

Originally published as 'Le séquestré de Venise' in *Situations IV* (Paris: Gallimard, 1964), pp. 291–346.

First published in English translation in *Portraits* (London: Seagull Books, 2009), pp. 231–516.

'A Fine Display of Capuchins'

Originally published as 'Un parterre de capucines' in *Situations IV* (Paris: Gallimard, 1964), pp. 435–43.

First published in English translation in *Portraits* (London: Seagull Books, 2009), pp. 642–54.

'Venice from My Window'

Originally published as 'Venise de ma fenêtre' in *Situations IV* (Paris: Gallimard, 1964), pp. 444–59.

First published in English translation in *Portraits* (London: Seagull Books, 2009), pp. 655–76.